Interruption and Imagination

Interruption and Imagination

PUBLIC THEOLOGY IN TIMES OF CRISIS

Kjetil Fretheim

◆PICKWICK *Publications* · Eugene, Oregon

INTERRUPTION AND IMAGINATION
Public Theology in Times of Crisis

Copyright © 2016 Kjetil Fretheim. All rights reserved. Except for brief quotations in critical publications or reviews, no part of this book may be reproduced in any manner without prior written permission from the publisher. Write: Permissions, Wipf and Stock Publishers, 199 W. 8th Ave., Suite 3, Eugene, OR 97401.

Pickwick Publications
An Imprint of Wipf and Stock Publishers
199 W. 8th Ave., Suite 3
Eugene, OR 97401

www.wipfandstock.com

PAPERBACK ISBN: 978-1-4982-9868-1
HARDCOVER ISBN: 978-1-4982-5615-5
EBOOK ISBN: 978-1-4982-9869-8

Cataloguing-in-Publication data:

Names: Fretheim, Kjetil.

Title: Interruption and imagination : public theology in times of crisis / Kjetil Fretheim.

Description: Eugene, OR : Pickwick Publications, 2016 | Includes bibliographical references.

Identifiers: ISBN 978-1-4982-5615-5 (paperback) | ISBN 978-1-4982-9868-1 (hardcover) | ISBN 978-1-4982-9869-8 (ebook)

Subjects: LCSH: Church and the world. | Common good—Religious aspects—Christianity. | Christians—Political activity. | Religion and politics.

Classification: BT738 .F65 2016 (paperback) | BT738 .F65 (ebook)

Manufactured in the U.S.A.   12/15/16

Contents

Preface | vii

1 Challenged by Crisis | 1
2 The Public Sphere | 14
3 Public Theology | 32
4 Times of Crisis | 59
5 Social Analysis | 74
6 Politics and Ethics | 94
7 Language and Voice | 114
8 The Climate Crisis | 132
9 Responding to Crisis | 141
  Conclusion | 155

Bibliography | 159

Preface

In the early 1990s the Berlin wall had just fallen, the Cold War had come to an end, and South Africa had been freed from the burden of apartheid. This was "the end of history"[1] and the hopes for a new era of democracy, human rights, and good governance were high. Soon, however, it became clear that the 1990s would not be the decade of peace and prosperity we had hoped for. Saddam Hussain invaded Kuwait and the United States (and others) went to war. Later Somalia collapsed, as did Yugoslavia. In Rwanda the international community passively witnessed brutal massacres and genocide. The dramatic events of 9/11 in 2001 defined the following decade and paved the way for the so-called war on terror, with the related invasion and war in Afghanistan. Later, Iraq became a new battleground. The Arab spring turned into a long, cold winter and as I am writing this the media keeps reporting about violence and brutal conflicts in Ukraine, Syria, and Yemen.

In times like these Christians despair, cry out, and attempt to assist. Some turn to religious resources in biblical texts and church tradition. Here they find words of pain, grief, and sorrow, and make them their own:

> Our LORD, how long must I beg
> for your help
> before you listen?
> How long before you save us
> from all this violence?
> Why do you make me watch
> such terrible injustice?
> Why do you allow violence,
> lawlessness, crime, and cruelty
> to spread everywhere?

1. Fukuyama, *End of History*.

Preface

> Laws cannot be enforced;
> justice is always the loser;
> criminals crowd out honest people
> and twist the laws around.²

These events of the last quarter of a century are paralleled by increased wealth for some and sustained poverty for others. The UN's recognition of "the inherent dignity and of the equal and inalienable rights of all members of the human family"³ has not prevented a world of inequality. Volatile markets, financial crisis, and austerity policies have been felt by banks and businesses, but not least by quite ordinary people, families, and local communities worldwide. On top of all of this, the climate crisis continues to threaten all of us, though some are likely to feel its effects more severely than others.

It is against this background of social, economic, political, and ecological crisis that this book addresses the practice and study of public theology. Public theology is committed to seeing, understanding, and interpreting these signs of the times, to proclaim hope and to make a difference. It seeks to inform and shape the political discourse and to find ways for positive change in local communities and society at large. The complexity of international relations, world economics, and the interplay between man, nature and society makes, however, the challenge of understanding what is going on a profoundly difficult one. The challenge becomes even greater if one not only seeks to understand what is going on, but also to change it. Public theology takes on this challenge.

Of course, public theology will always be colored by the perspective from which it is practiced. The same applies to this volume. It is written by a Norwegian and from a Northern European perspective. My socio-religious background is the Lutheran tradition within Christian thought and the close ties between the church and political authorities that characterize the Nordic countries. I also speak from the North, from a position of relative privilege and wealth, knowing that others live in a world of poverty, oppression, and marginalization. My interests, concerns, and commitment go, however, beyond the limits of my specific location. I live in a globalized community. We are all bound together in one international, global community of human beings and part of the one and same world: God's creation.

---

2. Hab 1:2–4, Contemporary English Version (CEV).
3. United Nations, "Universal Declaration of Human Rights," 353–58.

Preface

The following reflections on public theology are a result of a long-time fascination with contextual and socially committed theology both in the global South and in my own Northern European context. They are also a result of discussions with students at MF Norwegian School of Theology, in particular students of the MA-programs on Religion, Society and Global Issues and Diaconal studies. Parts of the following have been presented and discussed at the American Academy of Religion (AAR) and other scholarly conferences. Most of all, however, this book is a result of my one year sabbatical at York St John University, UK. I want to thank Professor Sebastian Kim in particular for making my stay as a visiting scholar possible and for engaging discussions on public theology.

The sabbatical in York was a unique experience not only in academic terms, but also for my family. I thank my wife Jenny for her support and Wednesday lunches.

1

Challenged by Crisis

There seems to be no end to the violent conflicts, oppression, and injustice in the world. Aid organizations keep sending out appeals in response to emergency situations and chronic poverty. Amnesty International continues to present brutal evidence of human rights violations and the International Crisis Group must carry on their work to prevent and resolve deadly conflict. In the midst of this turmoil the global community is faced with unprecedented climate change and its dire consequences. Global warming is a reality and we can see the effects of extraordinarily strong storms and hurricanes, floods, and drought. Some people, even some nation-states, find their livelihood and very existence threatened. Others struggle with changing weather patterns, seeking ways to cope and care for each other in new and unknown climate conditions.

Crises such as these call for action, but also deep reflection. How did we get to this point? What choices should we make now and how can we shape a better future?

The climate crisis illustrates the complexity of these questions. This is evidently an ecological crisis, but not only that. Climate change is caused by the wealth, consumption, and lifestyles of the rich, but also by the polluting industries and limited resources of poor countries. This makes the climate crisis not only an ecological or economic issue, but also a political challenge. New policies at all levels—local, national and global—are needed. This is no small task, but it must be done. In fact, it is an existential challenge. People's lives are at risk. Living in despair and feeling hopeless, people ask the obvious, challenging, and disturbing questions: Why this suffering, and why me? Where is God in this crisis? The problem of evil becomes not only a philosophical riddle to solve, but a personal and collective struggle. It leads us into the abyss of suffering and meaninglessness, as well as to the imperative of care and compassion, and a fight for recovery, reconstruction, and reconciliation. The crisis presents us with not only an intellectual, political, and existential challenge. It becomes a moral commitment.

Although the contemporary climate crisis is of a scale and character that makes it unique in human history, these questions and challenges are not unprecedented. Most of us have faced crisis of some kind in our personal lives or in our families. Some of us have faced brutal conflict, terrorist attacks, and war. To the international community, two world wars and decades of cold war are defining events of our political history. They have involved political antagonism, a costly arms race, suffering, and death for far too many. These crises have challenged individuals, local communities, civil society groups, and politicians to respond with moral outrage, political vision, and new and creative policy measures. Similarly, political analysts, social scientists, and philosophers have been challenged to analyze, reflect, and reconsider. How should we respond to such crises? What can we say, and what can we do?

Different groups of people, communities, and countries have given different answers to these questions. This book deals with how churches and Christians—clergy, theologians, and lay people—can respond to them. In other words, the aim is to explore the shape, form, and meaning of public theology in times of crisis. Accordingly, the book is about theology, but not theology in general. It focuses on a specific kind of theological approach or theological enterprise: the kind of theology that intentionally and explicitly deals with issues of public concern and seeks to participate in the public debates on such issues.

CRISES AND CHRISTIANITY

The Christian heritage with regard to world poverty, human rights violations, terrorism, war, and other forms of social and political crises, is a mixed one. Some see in religion in general and Christianity in particular a key contributing factor to crises. Christianity causes conflict, legitimizes hierarchy, and justifies oppression, it is claimed. Others point out how Christians and Christian churches have responded to historical crisis with love, care, and the message of Christian hope.

What seems clear is that crises have challenged and indeed changed Christian theology. The First World War challenged the optimism of European liberal theology and paved the way for a turn to God's transcendence in Christian theology and a much more skeptical and realistic understanding of contemporary culture. The Second World War saw the complicity as well as quietist attitude of churches and Christians, resulting in heated debates in the following decades. The state of Israel was established in 1948 partly with the support of Christian churches. Later the same churches have become increasingly aware of the disturbing effects of Israeli policies and the plight of Palestinians. In South Africa the Dutch Reformed Church developed a theological legitimation of an appalling apartheid system that was later condemned as heretical by other churches.

These examples indicate how churches, Christian theology, clergy, and Christians have been part of the problem, both through complicity and passivity. There are, however, also examples of how churches and Christians have responded publicly, critically, and constructively to social and political crises. Brave Christians in the Confessional Church spoke out against the Nazi regime. New theological understandings of the Promised Land have been developed, questioning both Christian Zionism and the policies of the international community in the Middle East. For decades churches and Christians have addressed poverty, racism, imperialism, and economic exploitation.

Today the global community and the ecumenical fellowship of all churches are challenged by climate change. Again one of the issues is how Christianity is part of the problem,[1] but churches and Christians have also developed new forms of theologies and are searching for creative ways of dealing with the crisis. Christian interpretations and viewpoints are articulated in the public sphere with an implicit or explicit understanding of climate change and its moral and political implications.

PUBLIC THEOLOGY

Such responses to climate change are examples of public theology in as much as they are articulated as theologically informed statements in the public sphere. Similarly, public statements given by churches, church officials, or ordinary Christians on economic exploitation, political oppression, or climate change are examples of public theology in practice. When

---

1. White, "Historical Roots," 1203–7.

they are examined and scrutinized by scholars they become the material and starting point for the academic field of public theology. The term public theology thus refers to both a practice and an academic discipline. To the extent that public theology scholars make their own contributions of this kind, they act as practical-public theologians.

As the North American theologian Robert Benne puts it, public theology is "the *engagement* of a living religious tradition with its public environment—the economic, political, and cultural spheres of our common life."[2] Similarly, Harold Breitenberg defines public theology as "theologically informed public discourse about public issues, addressed to the church, synagogue, mosque, temple, or other religious body, as well as the larger public or publics, argued in ways that can be evaluated and judged by publicly available warrants and criteria."[3] These definitions indicate what public theology is all about, but both Benne and Breitenberg also provide more elaborate definitions. Benne identifies two poles—religion and society (which consists of economic, political and cultural spheres)—and argues that "the vast majority of religious traditions not only intend to exist within and interact with them, but also aim to affect those public spheres."[4] This aim to affect leads the religious traditions to engage in the public environment. Further, Benne highlights two ways in which a religious or theological intellectual tradition engages the public world:

> First, that intellectual tradition moves outward from the tradition toward the world. It *interprets* the public world in light of the religious tradition. (. . .) Moreover, the intellectual tradition may be used to *persuade* the world of the cogency of its vision of how things ought to be in the public spheres of life. That is, there may be an apologetic thrust in the tradition. (. . . Second, the) world is interpreted and assessed by its teachers and scholars for the use of the tradition itself. (. . .) The tradition needs to clarify the character of the world so that it might resist where it needs to and adapt where it can. An interpretation of the world must be brought back to the tradition for the sake of its own integrity. At times this

---

2. Benne, *Paradoxical Vision*, 4, original emphasis. The term public theology can be used in many different ways. A good overview can be found in Breitenberg, "To Tell the Truth," 55–96. For a more recent discussion, see Jacobsen, "Models of Public Theology," 7–22.

3. Breitenberg, "To Tell the Truth," 66.

4. Benne, *Paradoxical Vision*, 7.

interpretation of the world may mean a critique and revision of the tradition itself.[5]

Breitenberg's longer definition of public theology has three parts:

> First, public theology is religiously informed discourse that intends to be intelligible and convincing to adherents within its own religious tradition while at the same time being comprehensible and possibly persuasive to those outside it. Second, public theology addresses issues that bear upon a religious community but also pertain to the larger society, including those who identify themselves with other faith traditions or with none. Third, to achieve such ends, public theology relies on sources of insight, language, methods of augment, and warrants that are in theory open to all.[6]

This concern and focus on "the larger society" is also reflected in the Scottish theologian Duncan B. Forrester's approach to public theology. Forrester argues public theology is a "theology which is not primarily concerned with individual subjectivity, or with the internal discourse of the Church about doctrine and its clarification" and consequently different from "evangelical theology which addresses the Gospel to the world in the hope of repentance and conversion."[7] Rather, public theology is a:

> theology which seeks the welfare of the city before protecting the interests of the Church, or its proper liberty to preach the Gospel and celebrate the sacraments. Accordingly, public theology often takes 'the world's agenda', or parts of it, as its own agenda, and seeks to offer distinctive and constructive insights from the treasury of faith to help in the building of a decent society, the restraint of evil, the curbing of violence, nation-building, and the reconciliation in the public arena, and so forth.[8]

Forrester thus distinguishes between the church and the city (drawing on Augustin's distinction between the eternal city of God and the temporal city of man[9]), and relates public theology in particular to the latter. Making "the world's agenda" the agenda of public theology is, however, not to do away with the theological identity and character of public theology. In

---

5. Ibid., 8, original emphasis.
6. Breitenberg, "To Tell the Truth," 65–66.
7. Forrester, "Scope of Public Theology," 6.
8. Ibid., 6.
9. Augustine, *Confessions*.

fact, the aim of public theology is to make use of theological concepts and insights to assess and consider life in the world. Thus, Forrester can also describe public theology as a form of God-talk with the ambition of speaking in a manner accessible and relevant to the world. Forrester says public theology is:

> talk about God, which claims to point to publicly accessible truth, to contribute to public discussion by witnessing to a truth that is relevant to what is going on in the world and to the pressing issues which are facing people and societies today (. . .) It takes the public square and what goes on there seriously, but it tries to articulate in the public square its convictions about truth and goodness. It offers convictions, challenges and insights derived from the tradition of which it is a steward, rather than seeking to articulate a consensus or reiterate what everyone is saying anyway.
>
> Public theology is thus confessional and evangelical. It has a gospel to share, good news to proclaim. Public theology attends to the Bible and the tradition of faith at the same time as it attempts to discern the sign of the times and understand what is going on in the light of the gospel.[10]

In other words, to Forrester, making the world's agenda one's own and adopting a theological perspective are fully compatible and at the core of public theology. It is by combining theological resources with a concern for the social, political, and economic conditions in the world that public theology seeks to understand the signs of the times.

This concern for "the welfare of the city"[11] and the social and economic conditions of the world makes public theology not simply about seeking understanding and contributing to a discussion. As Breitenberg points out, Christian public theology not only "intends to provide theologically informed interpretations of and guidance for individuals, faith communities, and the institutions and interactions of civil society, in ways that are understandable, assessable, and possibly convincing to those inside the church and those outside as well," but also "in so doing possibly persuade and move to action both Christians and non-Christians."[12] Similarly, the German theologian and Lutheran bishop Heinrich Bedford-Strohm explicitly relates public theology to politics:

---

10. Forrester, *Truthful Action*, 127–28.
11. Jer 29:7, New Revised Standard Version (NRSV).
12. Breitenberg, "To Tell the Truth," 66.

> If theology is not understood as the internal sign system for a closed religious community but as public theology, that is, as a theology which addresses the world as a whole, it has a natural closeness to questions of politics; that is, to the search of binding rules for living together in this world.[13]

This political dimension of public theology raises the question of the relationship between public theology on the one hand and decision making and policy implementation on the other hand. South African theologian Nico Koopman addresses this issue by posing a set of four questions:

> (a) What is the exact role of religion in public policy discourse, i.e., does religion only provide a motivation, goal and meaning, giving a framework for debates on policy, or does religion make a unique and indispensable input regarding the contents of the debate? (. . .) (b) If religion makes a contribution on the material, substantial level, what should the format of those contents be, i.e., broad visions, values and principles, or blueprints for decisions and policies? (. . .) (c) What is the role of the most vulnerable in society in the policy discourse? (d) What is the role of churches regarding the implementation of policies?[14]

Public theology gives different answers to these questions, but they remind us of the close connection that can be made between public theology, political issues, and policy making.

To sum up, public theology shares with other forms of theology an interest in expressing the Christian faith. It is committed to the Christian tradition and seeks to interpret the meaning and implications of this tradition in the contemporary world and to offer theologically informed contributions to the public sphere. This makes public theology not only a critical, but also a constructive, exercise. As a field of scholarly inquiry, public theology's aim is a better practice of such public participation by churches and Christians.

PROBLEMS OF PUBLIC THEOLOGY

The roots of public theology can be traced back to the early days of Christianity, but my interest here is public theology in the present. As we live in times of climate change and other crises, contemporary, public theology

---

13. Bedford-Strohm, "Public Theology and Political Ethics," 273–274.
14. Koopman, "Churches and Public Policy," 44.

must seek to understand the challenges of the day and to find ways of dealing with them. Both the practice and study of public theology in the present come, however, with considerable challenges and public theologians disagree about many issues. They differ over sources of insight and how they are used, the contents and the particulars of the analysis, as well as the conclusions and policy proposals put forward.

Given the huge task of understanding society in a period of vast inequalities, social injustice, war, and conflict in all its complexity, this is not surprising. The challenge remains profound even if one focuses on wealthy and presumed peaceful parts of the world. My home country, Norway, is one of the richest and most peaceful countries in the world, but on 22 July 2011 Norway experienced the most brutal and violent attacks in its peace time history. A young man, born and raised in Norway, culturally, religiously, and ethnically a member of the majority community in the country, killed 77 individuals, mostly young people participating in a camp organized by the youth wing of the social-democratic party. Against this background, how should one describe Norwegian society? What are its main characteristics and challenges? Scholars, politicians and news commentators all over the world struggle with similar questions and give many and diverging answers. This is the challenge of social analysis and an important part of public theology: How can we make sense of society? How should we read the signs of the times?

The pessimist might think that contemporary society is characterized by social and moral decay and argue in a retrospective and naive way that everything was better in "the good old days." The optimist, on the other hand, points to the technological advances we have seen in the last decades, increased wealth and welfare and thinks it is reasonable to expect similar advances in the future too. In this perspective our time becomes a time of opportunity and improvement. Clearly, however, both of these types of social analysis have several problems.

Firstly, this kind of analysis is one-dimensional and lacks nuance. If social analysis is summarized in one word—be it decay or opportunity—it seems reasonable to ask if this is a characteristic fitting for all strata of society, people in different locations and with varying social, economic or political capital. Is it really the case that things were a lot better (or worse) in former times? Do all of us have the same opportunities to shape our lives and circumstances?

Secondly, historical change and progress might solve some problems, but they also tend to create new ones. While new opportunities are, on the one hand, an expression of increased freedom, they also create room for new processes and actions that need critical questioning. Nuclear and genetic technologies are obvious examples: technological advances have created new opportunities, but with obvious challenges associated with them. Even if we assume agreement on how to describe the current state, the normative assessment of it is not necessarily given.

Thirdly, social analysis is always contextual, provisional, and controversial. Accordingly, any social analysis must specify which society, which situation, and what group of people it aims to say something about. If we are theologians, social scientists, or ethicists, our analysis comes from the perspective of our personal, social, cultural, and academic backgrounds.

In addition, social analysis must always be open for new interpretations. It needs to be inter-subjective and to invite perspectives from different standpoints—i.e., from young and old, rich, and poor, people in the North and people in the South. Similarly, every social analysis needs to acknowledge the fact that society is in flux. The character of a given society thus needs to be (re)assessed, (re)analyzed, and criticized (again) at different points in time. And finally, in times of crisis the social analysis must provide answers that can assist those who are suffering. This includes a moral call for action. Something should be done about war, poverty, and climate change.

The complexity of these issues has led some churches and Christians into mute passivity. Often churches and Christians are in doubt about how they should respond to issues of the time—issues that are disputed not only in public debate, but also within the Christian tradition and the community of the church. What can be said from a faith-based perspective? How can theology provide resources and perspectives that constructively deal with these issues? Can a church be politically involved at all?

Others have resisted passivity and wanted to address these issues, but have been faced with a set of further challenges. Not only the question of what they should say, but also how they should say it. Issues of social concern are often dealt with in the language of politics, technocratic bureaucracy, or secular reason, but this is not intuitively the primary language of the church. When discussing these issues as religious individuals or communities of faith, the language of faith, Scripture, and the particular religious tradition is often an important resource and point of reference. This shapes the religious understanding and interpretation of the issues at hand. But how can, or should, this be conveyed in the public sphere? In what way should public contributions be not only implicitly, but even explicitly informed by religious perspectives and resources?

As a theological commitment to address, communicate, and be in dialogue with a broad public sphere, public theology needs to find the right balance. It must draw on its particular religious tradition, but speak to all. Public theology must make use of its theological resources: the Christian texts, tradition, and faith community, but also be informed by insights and perspectives from other fields of study and inquiry. And, public theology must speak with a vision of a better future for all, but at the same time acknowledge the restrictions and limitations that frame actual political decision making.

My aim in this book is to develop an understanding of public theology and how it can find its role and identity in a balanced combination of such concerns, traditions, and language in times of crisis. More specifically I will focus on three problems of public theology. First, what should public theology say about social issues in times of crisis? Second, what kind of political and moral actions should public theology recommend? and third: how should public theology express its perspectives and concerns? These are the problems of 1) social analysis, 2) politics and ethics, and 3) language and voice.

All of these questions and problems come with no quick-fix answers. Rather, the answers to them seem to lie in a reasoned and well balanced reflection on the character of the issues at hand and the context in which they appear and in which the faith community finds it place. Considered answers rely not least on the informed interpretation of religious faith, scriptures, and tradition as well as a nuanced discernment of the signs of the times and the problems people face in their everyday lives.

STRUCTURE AND ARGUMENT

In this book, I approach these problems of public theology by first examining the concept of "the public sphere" as this has been expounded by scholars such as the German philosopher Jürgen Habermas, the American philosopher and political scientist Nancy Fraser, and others. I note that the understanding of the public sphere as a free, open space for equal participation by everyone is an ideal notion and contrasts with the restricted public sphere in real life. In addition I make the point that the public sphere today cannot be understood exclusively as a local or national sphere, but is simultaneously local, national, and global. I then move on to describe the socio-cultural context of this public sphere, drawing on the notions of secularism and the post-secular society, as well as postmodernity and pluralism. Chapter 2 closes with a discussion of the role of religion in the public sphere. I argue that there is a role for religion to play in the public sphere, and that this is both a descriptive and a normative claim. Religion is already at play, and religious perspectives should be made transparent and explicit in public debates.

In chapter 3 I revisit the concept of public theology. I argue that public theology is not only theologically justified, but has the Christian faith as its theological foundation. The question why Christians, churches, or clergy should participate in debates in the public sphere is answered with reference to the universal character of the Christian faith: God having created every human being and the whole of creation, Jesus' ministry to all, and the continued re-creation and presence of God in the world through the Holy Spirit. I then trace the development of public theology through the last century and consider how public theology can be understood and practiced in different ways. I also present Robert Benne's proposal for a theological-ethical framework for public theology characterized by a "paradoxical vision." I close chapter 3 by highlighting some of the key features of public theology.

In chapter 4 I discuss how crisis represents a specific challenge to public theology and how Christians have responded to crisis in three very different contexts: South Africa in the mid-1980s, the global South in the late 1980s, and in Palestine at the beginning of the new millennium. In all these cases Christians came together and produced written documents to address what the authors' saw as the crisis and challenges of their time. Considering these three documents I highlight the implications of understanding crisis as *kairos* and some of the perspectives and insights that follow from this approach in public theology.

Although there are sound theological reasons to engage in the public discourse with faith-based contributions and perspectives, this does not answer the question of how public theology should analyze and understand current social issues and concerns. Accordingly, in chapter 5 I address the problem of social analysis in public theology by examining the social analysis of kairos theology. This leads to a discussion of the relationship between theology and social analysis and I conclude by considering the interdisciplinary connections between these fields and how they can come together in public theology.

In chapter 6 I address the problem of politics and ethics in public theology. The question is not 'What to say?', but 'What to do?' First I examine the politics and ethics of kairos theology. I then contrast this with other approaches such as the public theology of Benne and the notion of middle axioms. I argue that public theology becomes political when theologically informed contributions in the public sphere address political issues or social concerns. In such cases political and ethical considerations become an important part of public theology.

Closely related to the question of what you want to say in the public debate, is the issue of how you want to say it. This issue of language and voice in public theology is considered in chapter 7. I first examine the language and voice of kairos theology and highlight the use of biblical language and theological terminology. Then I use the case of land—more specifically what is referred to as the Holy land, the Promised land, or God's land— to consider the prospects and pitfalls of religious language in the public sphere. I argue kairos theology suggests a creative, hybrid, and polyphonic way of expressing public theology through the use of different theological moods and moral discourses.

In chapter 8 I give an account of different responses to the ecological crisis and contemporary climate change and outline how a kairos inspired understanding of public theology can be applied to these issues.

In chapter 9 I reconsider the character of public theology in light of the preceding discussion. I argue that the kairos documents exemplify how theologically informed contributions to the public sphere are crucial to the public debate and can make a unique contribution to the public sphere. Public theology must be understood as a theological inquiry that seeks to interpret the crisis of the day, assess the moral and political implications, and outline ways to respond to these in practice. I conclude that the combination of theology, social theory, and ethics enables a creative, critical and productive analysis.

In particular I highlight how public theology can challenge the dominant discourses and implicit understandings in current debates. I call this the task of interruption. By interrupting the ongoing discourse, public theology can challenge widespread notions, presumptions, and the social imaginary,[15] and give resources for people to envisage a different discourse

---

15. Taylor, *Modern Social Imaginaries*.

and imagine a different kind of social reality. I also argue this is a constructive contribution to the public exchange. By interrupting, public theology offers new, alternative concepts, perspectives, and interpretations that challenge and expand the imagination. In other words, the role of public theology is to interrupt the flow of political exchange in the public sphere and to offer new imaginative interpretations of the present and alternative visions of the future.

Chapter 10 offers a short summary and conclusion.

2

The Public Sphere

Public theology focuses on the "welfare of the city" and the common good of all members of "the larger society." Theologically informed contributions to debates in the public sphere are both its task and aim.

In this chapter I address the issue of how *public* should be understood. I will discuss the origins and characteristics of the public sphere, but also nuance a uniform and monolithic understanding of this sphere by emphasizing its heterogeneity and pluralistic character. Accordingly, I will distinguish between different kinds of publics and the glocal character of the contemporary public sphere. Further, I will consider the broader cultural, social, economic, and political context of the(se) public sphere(s), highlighting the post-modern and post-secular character of contemporary society. The chapter closes with a consideration of the role of religion in the public sphere.

AN OPEN PUBLIC SPACE

Habermas has described and discussed the concept of the public sphere at length in his book *The Structural Transformation of the Public Sphere*.[1] Here he traces the origins of what we today refer to as the public sphere during the Enlightenment period and the modernization and emerging secularization of European society. This included the development of a bourgeois middle class. Habermas explains how members of the bourgeoisie would

1. Habermas, *Structural Transformation*.

read newspapers, meet in tea rooms and around coffee tables, and discuss issues of shared public and political concern. Thus, a space that was separate from the domestic, private sphere emerged and a modern form of public sphere was created. In the sense that they did not take part in the debate in some kind of official capacity, those participating in this public sphere were private persons. To Habermas, however, although private interests belong to the private and pre-political, they can be transformed and transcended through this kind of public debate.

As the Canadian philosopher Charles Taylor puts it, the people involved in this space were linked in a common space of discussion:

> Books, pamphlets, and newspapers circulated among the educated public, conveying theses, analyses, arguments, and counterarguments, referring to and refuting each other. These were widely read and often discussed in face-to-face gatherings, in drawing rooms, coffeehouses, salons, and in more (authoritatively) public places, like Parliament.[2]

Taylor calls this local space of discussion a "topical common space," but argues that something new emerges in the eighteenth century: a public sphere that ties together several such spaces. As it transcends the locality of the topical common space, Taylor describes this nonlocal common space as "metatopical."[3]

This was also a time when Christendom and the rule of a divine sovereign prince or monarch were challenged, not least by Enlightenment thinkers such as Grotius and Locke. Rather than basing political authority on divine command or inspiration, they focused on the individual human being and the social contract individuals make between themselves and the governing authorities. This meant that political authority came to be based on popular, rather than divine, authority. The will of the people would emerge through the exchange between individuals and through their public discourse. In Taylor's terminology: in the metatopical public sphere.

Taylor sums up the novelty of this larger space with two features. Firstly, this metatopical public sphere is independent from the political sphere. It is prepolitical and stands mentally outside of the polity. Secondly, it is based on the freedom and consent of its participants and a place for discussion and debate that should guide government. This implies that it is necessary to distinguish between the public discourse in the public sphere

2. Taylor, *Modern Social Imaginaries*, 84.
3. Ibid., 86.

and the political discourse of decision making. Taylor explains this distinction with a reference to the functioning of the ancient republic or polis. In the latter, the

> "unofficial" discussions are not separated off, given a status of their own, and seen to constitute a kind of metatopical space. But that is what happens with the modern public sphere. It is a space of discussion that is self-consciously seen as being outside power. It is supposed to be listened to by power, but it is not itself an exercise of power.[4]

Accordingly, the modern public sphere is distinguished from the sphere of public authority. It is, however, linked to the political sphere in as much as governments are considered obliged to listen to the discussion and to base their policies and actions on the consensus that emerges through discussion in the public sphere. Thus the public sphere, while in this sense extra-political, keeps political power in check.

In other words, this time in the words of the Spanish sociologist Manuel Castells, the public sphere is "the space where people come together as citizens and articulate their autonomous views to influence the political institutions of society."[5] In this way, the public sphere becomes the "cultural/informational repository of the ideas and projects that feed public debate."[6] Since citizens discuss issues of political importance, contributing to debates in the public sphere can also be described as a form of popular political participation.

Habermas argues the public sphere was created by the recognition of three sets of rights: Firstly, the right of radical freedom of speech and opinion, the free press, and freedom of assembly. This allowed for critical debate and political representation. Secondly, the right to personal freedom and the inviolability of the home, and third, the right of private ownership which required equality before the law.[7] These freedoms and rights imply that the public sphere should be an egalitarian arena inclusive to all. Differences in status, gender, ethnicity, sexual orientation, religious conviction etc. should be seen as irrelevant and disregarded. If some or specific groups were to be *eo ipso* excluded from this space, it would be less than complete

---

4. Ibid., 89.
5. Castells, "New Public Sphere," 78.
6. Ibid., 79.
7. Habermas, *Structural Transformation*, 83–85.

and no longer a public sphere.[8] Thus, this open space is an arena for conversation, dialogue, and rational discussion between everyone who wants to be part of it. It is "a network for communicating information and points of view"[9] and a space where citizens discuss issues they have in common. Rational and critical debate and common concerns should be the guiding focus of the discussion and the commitment of the participants.[10]

It is worth noting, however, that Habermas' discussion of the public sphere is largely developed in terms of ideal types. The strength of ideal theory is that it helps us focus on the key features of general phenomena and to highlight the moral concerns that should govern them. However, ideal notions rarely match real life circumstances. In fact, the particular, organized, and material expressions of the public sphere vary historically and contextually.[11] Its characteristics and position in relation to other publics also appear in several different ways.

COMPETING PUBLICS

One of the key critiques of Habermas' understanding of the public sphere comes from feminist scholars. They have challenged the distinction he makes between the public, the private, and the political, and pointed out how the public sphere in real life is far from being as open as Habermas describes it.

One of these critics is Nancy Fraser. She is sympathetic to Habermas' analysis, but argues it "needs to undergo some critical interrogation and reconstruction if it is to yield a category comparable of theorizing the limits of actually existing democracy."[12] In this way, she seeks to respond both to the criticism of Habermas' theory for being too idealistic, and to the fact that it is developed in relation to the bourgeois society in modern, Western Europe. Fraser identifies and examines four assumptions underlying the bourgeois conception of public sphere and then points towards an alternative understanding of the public sphere.

---

8. Ibid., 85.
9. Habermas, *Between Facts and Norms*, 360.
10. Habermas, *Structural Transformation*, 72. For more on the public sphere, see Calhoun, *Habermas*; Goode, *Jürgen Habermas*; Smit, "Notions of the Public"; and Gripsrud et al., *Idea of the Public Sphere*.
11. Castells, "New Public Sphere."
12. Fraser, "Rethinking the Public Sphere," 57.

Firstly, she challenges the assumption that societal equality is not a necessary condition for political democracy. In other words, while Habermas' approach relies on the notion that all the (unequal) participants can be considered equal, Fraser is much more concerned about actual differences and inequalities in real life situations. While Habermas wants to bracket social inequalities, Fraser argues that "such bracketing usually works to the advantage of dominant groups in society and to the disadvantage of subordinates."[13] Fraser's alternative is to make such inequalities explicit.

Secondly, Fraser addresses the assumption that the proliferation of a multiplicity of competing publics is necessarily a step away from, rather than toward, greater democracy and that a single, comprehensive public sphere is always preferable to a nexus of multiple publics. Thus, while Habermas is concerned with the public sphere in the singular, Fraser writes about plural publics and counter publics.[14] She argues that "the idea of an egalitarian, multi-cultural society only makes sense if we suppose a plurality of public arenas in which groups with diverse values and rhetorics participate. By definition, such a society must contain a multiplicity of publics."[15]

Not only are there several publics, they are also not ideal entities but "formed under conditions of dominance and subordination."[16] Fraser argues the subaltern counter publics "are parallel discursive arenas where members of subordinated social groups invent and circulate counter discourses, which in turn permit them to formulate oppositional interpretations of their identities, interests, and needs."[17] Still, these counter publics are not enclaves, but have a publicist orientation and stay in touch with the wider publics, the "public-at-large." She points out that "people participate in more than one public, and that the memberships of different publics may partially overlap."[18]

Thirdly, Fraser examines the assumption that discourse in public spheres should be restricted to deliberation about the common good, and that the appearance of "private interests" and "private issues" is always undesirable. She notes that Habermas' notion of the public arena as a place where "private persons" deliberate about "public matters" implies several

13. Ibid., 64.
14. See also Warner, *Publics and Counterpublics*.
15. Fraser, "Rethinking the Public Sphere," 69.
16. Ibid., 70.
17. Ibid., 67.
18. Ibid., 70.

The Public Sphere

different senses of privacy and publicity. "Publicity" can mean 1) state-related; 2) accessible to everyone; 3) of concern to everyone; or 4) pertaining to a common good or shared interest. Each of these corresponds to a contrasting sense of "privacy." In addition, there are two other senses of "privacy" at play: "5) pertaining to private property in a market economy; and 6) pertaining to intimate domestic or personal life, including sexual life."[19] In this way, Fraser makes the point that "[w]hat will count as a matter of common concern will be decided precisely through discursive contestation. It follows that no topics should be ruled off limits in advance of such contestation."[20]

Fourthly and finally, Fraser addresses "the assumption that a functioning democratic public sphere requires a sharp separation between civil society and the state."[21] Habermas sees the public sphere as a counterweight to the state, and "it is precisely this extra-governmental character of the public sphere that confers an aura of independence, autonomy, and legitimacy on the "public opinion" generated in it."[22] While the public sphere is an open space for the exchange of viewpoints, interpretations, and arguments, the political sphere is where decisions are made. Politicians and bureaucrats are the decision makers who must assess the facts and the arguments put forward, and, according to their own judgement, decide what policies should be implemented. They do not have the outsider's privilege of observing and criticizing, but need to act on the information they have and decide how to approach the future.

This is the difference between discussion and decision, as noted above, and it is in this context that Fraser makes a distinction between weak and strong publics. The weak publics are "publics whose deliberative practice consists exclusively in opinion-formation and does not also encompass decision-making."[23] With popular and parliamentary sovereignty the public became both opinion forming and decision making. This is what she calls a strong public.

19. Ibid., 70–71.
20. Ibid., 71.
21. Ibid., 63.
22. Ibid., 75.
23. Ibid., 75.

INTERRUPTION AND IMAGINATION

GLOBALIZATION AND GLOCALIZATION

Theologically informed contributions to the public sphere can be, and are being, articulated in and around the tables of coffee shops and restaurants in places where people live their everyday lives. The notion of a public sphere relies, however, on the imagined community that goes beyond face-to-face encounters in coffee shops and restaurants. Given the development of communication means across longer distances and the related political nation-states, one such imagined community is the nation and the corresponding national public sphere.[24] The role of the nation-state is, however, being challenged and changed by the various processes of globalization.[25] Accordingly, it is necessary to also consider the global dimensions of the public sphere.

Globalization can be understood as the "process that constitutes a social system with the capacity to work as a unit on a planetary scale in real or chosen time."[26] Castells describes this capacity as threefold: technological, institutional, and organizational. In the age of globalization, information and communication technologies enable the exchange of people, goods, and ideas both rapidly and across long distances. Information technology makes it possible to address common issues on a global scale, addressing concerns and challenges across political, cultural, and religious borders. At the same time the nation-state's control over territory and citizens is reduced, leading to deregulation, liberalization, privatization, and weakened institutional capacity. Finally, organizational capacity is "the ability to use networking as the flexible, interactive, borderless form of structuration of whatever activity in whatever domain."[27] This implies a further broadening of communication and interaction between people far beyond the limits of local settings and national borders.

Castells deepens our understanding of globalization further by distinguishing between four different forms of organizations in global civil society: 1) local civil society actors; 2) non-governmental organizations (NGOs) with a global or international frame of reference in their actions and goals; 3) social movements that aim to control the process of

24. Anderson, *Imagined Communities*.

25. Eriksen, "Globalization."

26. Castells, "New Public Sphere," 81. For more on globalization, see Bauman, *Globalization*; Beck, *What Is Globalization?*; Scholte, *Globalization*; and Held and McGrew, *Globalization/Anti-Globalization*.

27. Castells, "New Public Sphere," 81.

The Public Sphere

globalization; and 4) the movement of public opinion. The first of these, local civil society actors, are strictly speaking not themselves part of a global civil society, but do constitute a "milieu of organization, projects, and practices that nurtures the growth of the global society."[28] The second category corresponds to what is often referred to as global civil society but focusses on international, private, non-governmental organizations such as Amnesty International, Médecins Sans Frontières, Oxfam, Greenpeace etc. These are organizations that affirm universally recognized values such as human rights and social justice. Castells point out three characteristics of this kind of organizations. Firstly, they have considerable popular support and benefit from both private donations and volunteerism. Secondly, their focus is not primarily on justifying policies or rationalizing decisions, but practical matters and concrete solidarity work: feeding the hungry, saving children, stopping poverty etc. Thirdly, these organizations use media politics to mobilize support for their cause.

Castell's third category concerns social movements that aim to control the process of globalization. These movements often referred to as the anti-globalization movement, establish "networks of action and organization to induce a global social movement for global justice."[29] The connections between such movements amount to a global network that is highly critical of the form and consequences of current globalization processes, calling for new forms of representation, global governance, and solidarity.

Finally, Castell's fourth expression of civil society is the movement of public opinion. This refers to the often "spontaneous, ad hoc mobilizations using horizontal, autonomous networks of communication"[30] on the internet and through social media such as Facebook, YouTube, and Twitter. Examples of such movements appeared in the peace demonstrations against the Iraqi war in early 2003, in the mobilization against the military regime in Myanmar in 2007, and in the so-called Arab-spring between 2010 and 2012.

Castells' analysis helps us recognize and acknowledge how processes of globalization generate not only a new global society, but even new public spaces.[31] As is indicated in the description of Castell's four categories, the "new public sphere" is closely related to global communication and media

28. Ibid., 84.
29. Ibid., 85.
30. Ibid., 86.
31. Volkmer, *Global Public Sphere*.

systems. In such a global public sphere, matters that are seemingly local can become not only national but even global issues. Similarly, global issues can become issues debated around coffee tables in local communities. This two-way process can been described as a process of glocalization: local processes affect the global level, and global processes affect the local level. The public sphere is neither exclusively local nor exclusively global, but dynamic and *glocal*.[32]

One example of this glocal dimension of the public sphere is the reactions that followed the publishing of the Norwegian author and journalist Åsne Seierstad's *The Bookseller of Kabul*.[33] Based on her fieldwork and experiences in Afghanistan and visits to both the shop and the home of a bookseller in Kabul, she wrote a novel. The book was published in Norwegian in relatively low numbers and aimed at the Norwegian public. Soon, however, word reached Afghanistan, or, put differently, the Norwegian public reached Afghanistan. The bookseller subsequently contacted Åsne Seierstad and the publisher, argued that the book was insulting and wanted parts of the manuscript changed. A heated debate and a series of court trials followed. One lesson learned seems to be that neither the Norwegian nor the Afghan public sphere should be seen in isolation from each other and their global context.

Accordingly, while some see in contemporary globalization the demise of the nation-state, a more reasonable approach seems to be to understand globalization processes as giving an increased relevance to the global sphere. This comes in addition to other levels in society, not simply at the expense of, and thus there is a dynamic relationship between the local, national, and global levels. We need to remind ourselves, however, that there is an underside to globalization—those who are negatively affected by these very processes. There is also an outside to globalization—those who are not included. The global market and the internet might be widely accessible, but to actually access them and to make use of them and to be able to participate in a global discourse in a global arena is not an option to all. Although globalization implies the bringing together of a wide number of people from almost all countries and communities in the world, the global public sphere is not an entirely open space.

This broadening of the public sphere also reminds us of the challenges and concerns that are common not only to local communities or

32. Robertson, *Globalization*.
33. Seierstad, *Bookseller of Kabul*.

The Public Sphere

nation-states, but to humanity as a whole. In light of the contemporary climate crisis we must include not only humanity, but also animals and the natural world: the whole of creation. What this broadening of scale does not do, however, is to help us specify in a more nuanced fashion the different types of discourses that find their place in these local, national, and global public spheres. In this perspective, to talk about *one* global public sphere is highly problematic.

POST-MODERN, POST-SECULAR, AND PRECARIOUS

Examining the public sphere also leads us to consider its broader cultural, social, economic, and political context. One way of approaching this is to say that we live in a modern world. In many ways this remains true, although the processes of modernization have impacted societies in different ways resulting in multiple modernities.[34] Further, immense criticism has been raised against modernity and the related Enlightenment thought, characterized by arrogant anthropocentrism, materialism, positivism, and secular rationalism. With this in mind, it seems more fitting to describe the present day as post-modern. In post-modernity the faith in one rationality and universal ethics is questioned, and the number of different rationalities, the contextual character and many versions of ethics, as well as narratives people live by, are emphasized and celebrated.[35]

An important aspect of modernity was secularization. The religious wars in Europe pushed religion to the periphery of public life and the science-based knowledge of the Enlightenment discredited religious explanations and authorities. A commonly held version of the secularization thesis argued that religion, in the time of industrialization and modernization, would be given a gradually reduced role in the public sphere.[36] Indeed, some find, and regret, that there seems to have been a:

> loss of confidence by the leadership of the religious traditions themselves in the efficacy of their own vision's capacity to contribute to public discourse. They often capitulate before the forces of secularization by supplanting their own vision's insights with

---

34. Eisenstadt, "Comparative Civilizations."
35. Lyotard, *Postmodern Condition*.
36. Berger, *Sacred Canopy*; Bruce, *Secularization*.

INTERRUPTION AND IMAGINATION

those from sources more acceptable to the secular despisers of religion.[37]

Scholars have, however, described and analyzed this process of secularization in different ways.[38] One of them, José Casanova, has identified three understandings of the term. Secularization can refer to the decline of religious belief and the replacement of religious explanations by scientific ones. Secondly, it can mean the process of differentiation of the religious sphere from other spheres of life, which liberate themselves from the shadow of the sacred canopy of religion. Thirdly, secularization points to the privatization of religious life. This means that religious belief and practice disappear from the public sphere. Though religion might live on in private contexts, it would not be considered relevant or legitimate in the public sphere.[39]

Charles Taylor also highlights three ways of understanding the changes related to secularization. Firstly, in a secularized society significant institutions are founded on reason rather than on faith. Secondly, there is a demise of religion and religious belief. There might still be believers around, but for the majority of the population, religion plays a minimal role in their lives. So far Taylor reiterates what several secularization scholars already have pointed out. The novel and more important contribution from Taylor in this regard is the third feature he identifies: the change in conditions of belief. In *A Secular Age*, he writes:

> The shift to secularity in this sense consists, among other things, of a move from a society where belief in God is unchallenged and indeed, unproblematic, to one in which it is understood to be one option among others, and frequently not the easiest to embrace. (. . .) (T)he change I want to define and trace is one which takes us from a society in which it was virtually impossible not to believe in God, to one in which faith, even for the staunchest believer, is one human possibility among others.[40]

Given this condition, that religious faith is "one human possibility among others," religious voices and contributions to the public sphere need to explain and possibly justify themselves in ways that were neither necessary

---

37. Benne, *Paradoxical Vision*, 17.

38. For further analysis and discussion of the role of religion in modern societies, see Bruce, *Secularization* and Vallier, *Liberal Politics*.

39. Casanova, *Public Religions*.

40. Taylor, "A Secular Age," 3.

The Public Sphere

nor expected in earlier and very different times. This is accompanied by increasingly reflexive religiosities, meaning "expressions of religious commitment shaped by an often anxious awareness of their status as vulnerable rather than stable and chosen rather than given."[41]

The notion that secularization and modernization processes eventually would make religion retract to the private sphere and largely irrelevant and a stranger in the public sphere, has, however, been strongly challenged and criticized. Several scholars have noted a resurgence of religion[42] and how religion seems to have become increasingly relevant in both domestic and international politics. They point to the re-enchantment of the world[43] and the return of God.[44] Graham Ward highlights a new visibility of religion in three forms: religious fundamentalism, deprivatization of religion, and the commodification of religion.[45]

It is against this background that Habermas, one of the prominent proponents of the secularization thesis, has reconsidered his position and become one of many scholars who now speak of the post-secular society.[46] This new post-secular condition implies that:

> The conventional demarcations of 'public' and 'private', 'secular' and 'religious' are breaking down, along with the protocols governing the nature of public discourse and civil activism in liberal democracies. It is not clear, for example, that non-theological reasoning is any the less subjective or partial than any other form of public discourse. Similarly, the expectation that only people of faith might 'bracket out' their deepest moral convictions is no longer viewed as the ideal condition for participation in political life—on the contrary, it is increasingly regarded as a restriction on the exercise of free citizenship.[47]

This is not to say, however, that religion has become uncontroversial. Neither postmodernity nor the post-secular is a return to Christendom. Faith has become an option, but religious statements are not necessarily

---

41. Hogue, "After the Secular," 356.
42. Kepel, *Revenge of God*.
43. McGrath, *Re-Enchantment of Nature*.
44. Micklethwait and Wooldridge, *God Is Back*.
45. Ward, *Politics of Discipleship*, 135–54.
46. Habermas, *Between Naturalism and Religion* and Habermas, "Notes on Post-Secular Society."
47. Graham, *Between a Rock and a Hard Place*, 65.

self-explanatory. They also come in different forms, rooted in and informed by as diverse traditions as Christianity, Islam, and Judaism, Hinduism, Buddhism, and others. The postmodern and post-secular society is a pluralist, multi-cultural, and multi-religious society.

Another, less cultural and more material and economic way to describe the world we live in, would focus on the living conditions of men and women on the planet. World development reports[48] and the evaluation reports on the millennium development goals,[49] provide an interesting overview of how people live and the challenges they face. Compared to earlier times, the increase in welfare, longevity, education, and access to health services is remarkable and undoubtedly positive. There is wealth in the world and many of us benefit from the welfare it provides us. This is, however, not the full story. There are too many who do not have access to or benefit from this wealth and welfare. The millennium development goals have reduced poverty but not eliminated it. People continue to suffer on a daily basis, be it in the Brazilian favelas, in the slums of Calcutta, or in European hospitals. People live precarious lives[50] and sit by the beds of their friends and families in pain and grieve the deaths of their loved ones. Countries such as DR Congo, Iraq, and Syria have been experiencing brutal conflicts for many years. They are countries in crisis and the international community is constantly faced with such conflicts and the challenge of how to respond to them. The climate crisis is another such challenge and arguably one of prime global importance. Post-modern irony and relativism cannot take away the pain and suffering in this time of multiple crises.

PUBLIC RELIGION

The reactions against Salman Rushdie's *Satanic Verses* in 1989, the Muhammed Cartoon-crisis in Danish and Norwegian media in 2005, and the more recent Charlie Hebdo attacks in Paris in January 2015 illustrate not only that there is a glocal public sphere, but also that it has a religious dimension. Religion features in violent conflicts, terrorist attacks, and identity politics around the world. How it appears and is used varies, however.

Some see in religion a source of meaning, moral norms, and social cohesion. As religious values protect and promote the dignity of all human

---

48. See www.worldbank.org/en/publication/wdr/wdr-archive.
49. See www.un.org/millenniumgoals/reports.shtml.
50. Butler, *Precarious Life*.

beings and the integrity of non-human animals as well as the environment, they embrace religion in the public sphere and acknowledge the positive contribution of religion in social life. Religions and religious actors can alleviate suffering, promote solidarity, and mobilize social and political involvement. To others religion is irrational, authoritarian, and divisive and they would like to see a public sphere void of religious expressions. Richard Rorty famously described religion as a conversation-stopper[51] but has later withdrawn this claim. He maintains, however, that religious references primarily belong to the private sphere and not in the public square. Consequently, the public role of religion remains controversial and disputed.[52]

In agreement with Habermas, John Rawls sees the public square as a space where everyone can participate. In *Political Liberalism*[53] he argues that this open, democratic discourse represents the epistemic foundation for a secular state and is based on human rationality. Accordingly, it is important to Rawls that contributions to the public discourse are accessible to all and that they do not rely on a *comprehensive doctrine* not shared by everyone. Religions are such comprehensive doctrines, and the implication is that the public and political role of religion should be limited. Of course, Rawls accepts that comprehensive doctrines can be the motivating or ideological background for public statements, but when making such statements, he argues these documents should remain bracketed from the public discussion. As public reason is secular and rational, comprehensive doctrines have no role to play in the public discourse.

In his book *Between Naturalism and Religion*[54] Habermas not only reconsiders his previous understanding of secularization, but also develops a different approach to the role of religion in the public sphere. A key concern is to acknowledge the persistent role of religion in social life, and Habermas therefore uses the concept of the post-secular to describe the world we live in and how people see themselves. In addition, he has a normative aim. He wants to say something about how people should understand themselves:

---

51. Rorty, *Philosophy and Social Hope*, 168–74.

52. Contributions to these debates can be found in Audi and Wolterstorff, *Religion in the Public Square*; Sweetman, *Why Politics Needs Religion*; McGraw, *Faith in Politics*; Butler, Mendieta, and Van Antwerpen, *Power of Religion*; Kim, *Theology in the Public Sphere*; Volf, *A Public Faith*; and Williams, *Faith in the Public Square*.

53. Rawls, *Political Liberalism*.

54. Habermas, *Between Naturalism and Religion*.

> the expression "postsecular" does not merely grant religious communities public recognition for their functional contribution to the reproduction of desirable motives and attitudes. The public consciousness of a postsecular society reflects, rather, a normative insight that has implications for political interactions between religious and nonreligious citizens. In the postsecular society, the conviction is gaining ground that the "modernization of public consciousness" affects and reflexively transforms religious and secular mentalities, though not simultaneously. Both sides can then take each other's contributions to controversial public debates seriously for cognitive reasons as well, assuming that they share an understanding of the secularization of society as a *complementary* learning process.[55]

Considering the role religion plays in how people shape their identities, tie social bonds, and find meaning in their lives, Habermas identifies an opportunity to learn from these religious traditions. In the post-secular religious participants should seek to articulate their concerns in a secular and rational style so that it more easily can be accessible to all. However, to expect that religious citizens bracket or translate their comprehensive doctrines while others do not, would constitute a special limitation on the part of the former. He also argues religious participants should seek to understand what their secular conversation partners are saying, but similarly that the secular participants should seek to understand what their religious partners are saying. Accordingly, the learning process should be a *complementary* learning process.

This learning opportunity is a key concern in Habermas' account of the post-secular. In the context of political decision making, however, the translation from religious to rational language remains a pre-condition for Habermas. This is his *institutional translation provisio*. As the state should be neutral, only secular rationalism is acceptable in the context of political institutions. Religious participants should translate what they want to say into a common, secular language. Habermas argues, however, that this should be acceptable, even to religious participants:

> Religious citizens can certainly acknowledge this 'institutional translation provisio' without having to split their identity into public and private parts the moment they participate in public discourses. They should therefore also be allowed to express and

---

55. Ibid., 111, original emphasis.

justify their convictions in a religious language even when they cannot find secular "translations" for them.[56]

Accordingly, Habermas finds that religious and theological contributions need to be welcomed in the public spheres. To reject them would be to exclude interpretations and perspectives that actors actually have and carry with them.[57] However, this comes with a responsibility for both the sender and recipient. The sender must seek to explain their religious or theological informed views or social analysis in a way that makes it available also for those who do not share the framework or do not know the interpretative frame from which this emerges. The recipient has also a responsibility. She must be open to listen to the particular contribution of the other: the concerns it seeks to protect, how this coincides with those of others or their own concerns, and how they might conflict. In other words, not only a willingness to listen but also an ability to listen is necessary. Where religious literacy is lacking, this becomes a profound challenge.

Another scholar who has argued in favor of religious participation and articulations in the public sphere is the Protestant theologian Miroslav Volf. In his book *A Public Faith* Volf draws on the works of the Calvinist philosopher Nicholas Wolterstorff and discusses the role of religion in societies with multiple communities.[58] In each of them people can coexist respectfully as one group or society, but these communities also present themselves to the wider community. Echoing Fraser, Volf thus presents a "consocial" model of how different groups in multi-cultural and multi-religious societies can co-exist in one society, but argues this should be supplemented with notions of shared identity and common ground across such divides. Volf gives a four step argument for why monotheistic faiths should support liberal democracy:

1. Because there is one God, all people are related to that one God on equal terms.
2. The central command of that one God is to love neighbors—to treat others as we would like them to treat us, as expressed in the Golden rule.

---

56. Ibid., 130.

57. For more on Habermas and religion, see Adams, *Habermas and Theology* and Calhoun, Mendieta, and Van Antwerpen, *Habermas and Religion*.

58. Volf, *A Public Faith*, 125.

3. We cannot claim any rights for ourselves and our group that we are not willing to give to others.

4. Whether as a stance of the heart or as outward practice, religion cannot be coerced.[59]

In this perspective the public engagement of Christians involves speaking in their idiom and accepting "pluralism as a political project."[60] To contribute in the public sphere, however, it is imperative that people of faith are able to communicate their religious convictions and religiously informed views in a comprehensible manner.

THE PUBLIC SPHERE IN TIMES OF CRISIS

As extraordinary circumstances tend to call for extraordinary measures, the notion of an open, egalitarian space can easily be challenged in times of crises. Dramatic floods, hurricanes, and drought demand a response that the emergency services might not be equipped for, and the war on terror has led to calls for new anti-terror legislation. Special times require exceptional responses. On the other hand, these very measures may threaten the distinct features of the public sphere. Freedom of speech and the freedom of assembly can become restricted. A propaganda war can limit the space for political debate and the force of the better argument might lose to the force of identity politics, stereotypes, and prejudice. Indeed, strong publics can become weak publics. In effect, times of crisis can easily become a crisis for the public sphere.

Accordingly, in particular in times of crisis, it is imperative to participate in the public sphere and to protect it as an arena to discuss the immediate challenges, root causes of the problems at hand, and visions for a new future. Through the discussions and debates in the public sphere, perspectives, concerns, challenges, and hopes are shared and articulated, and in turn made accessible to the people in power. Thus they are fed into not only the popular discussions, but also the political discourses. In this, religious actors—local churches, faith-based NGOs, and social movements—all have a task and opportunity to give their theologically informed contributions to protect the public sphere and the welfare of all.

---

59. Ibid., 126.
60. Ibid., 126.

Given the multifaceted and complex character of the glocal public sphere, however, both social analysis and discursive exchanges about social issues and concerns become equally complex and demanding. Competing interests and interpretation of the issues and challenges to be addressed only adds to the problem of social analysis in public theology. Similarly, questions regarding ways and means of improving society are not easily answered. Given the precarious lives people live and the suffering and injustice they experience, there is an obvious need to act. The inequality, oppression, and marginalization of contemporary society represent an acute challenge to public theology, but how one should respond remains unclear. Accordingly, the problem of politics and ethics in public theology remains a profound challenge.

Further, the public sphere of the twenty-first century invites a range of narratives and rationalities. The challenge to speak out is, therefore, paralleled by a call to listen closely to others and to be willing to learn from their perspectives and concerns. Equally, there is a need to consider how one expresses and articulates one's own concerns and perspectives. This is the problem of language and voice in public theology.

3

Public Theology

Whilst the public sphere is the context for public theology, it does not define public theology. As the English public theologian Elaine Graham puts it: "public theology is not simply concerned *about* the public, but concerns itself with a particular kind of theological method *in relation to* the public."[1] I suggest that public theology considers the character of the public sphere, but finds its identity by reflecting on what theology is and what it implies in the present context. In fact, the starting point for practicing, developing, and constantly reassessing public theology, is the public character of theology itself.

I begin this chapter by arguing that Christian faith is inherently public and that this dimension of the Christian faith drives theology into the public sphere. There is, and should be, an important interface between Christian theology and public life. Consequently the public sphere should be no stranger to churches, Christians, or theologians. Given that the public sphere is, or should be, open to all people of faith, religious leaders, churches, and theologians, they should take part in the public debate.

Further, I give an account of the history and criticism of public theology, and describe how its social location has expanded to include new participants and voices. I then seek to position public theology in relation to related disciplines. I argue there are close affinities between public theology and several other theological approaches. I continue by presenting Robert

---

1. Graham, *Between a Rock and a Hard Place*, 97, original emphasis.

Benne's framework for public theology[2] and, finally, I outline some of the distinct features of glocal public theology.

THEOLOGY AND THE PUBLIC

To some the term public theology might seem like a contradiction in terms. Is not theology something that relates to churches, congregations, and something for Christians or religious people, with no, or at least limited, relevance beyond such groups? To others it might seem like an unnecessary specification. Are not all kinds of theology public theology? How can reflection on a God who has created the universe, and who loves everyone and who speaks to everyone, not be public? I sympathize with the latter position in as much as I agree with the Reformed, German theologian Jürgen Moltmann who argues that there is no Christian theology without public relevance.[3]

Indeed, the public character of the Christian faith is evident not only in its many public expressions in terms of rituals, church institutions, Christian social work etc. It also has solid biblical foundations. That God created "the heavens and the earth," decided to "give life to all kinds of tame animals, wild animals, and reptiles," and made "humans to be like himself" (Gen 1) is a key element of the biblical narrative. God's creation is paralleled by God's love for his people. When the people of Israel were suffering as slaves, God came down "to rescue them from the Egyptians" (Exod 3). Indeed, love and justice are closely related. The prophets of the Old Testament spoke out against injustice, and called the political authorities to repent (Amos, Hosea). Later, and from a Christian point of view more importantly, Jesus taught his followers not only to "love the Lord your God with all your heart, soul, strength, and mind," but also to "love your neighbors as much as you love yourself" (Luke 10:27) including our enemies (Matt 5:44). Further, Jesus called his disciples to "go to the people of all nations" (Matt 28:19) and Paul explained to the people of Athens how God "gives life, breath, and everything else to all people" (Acts 17:25). In other words, the Christian faith, and by extension Christian theology, concerns the world and calls us to seek the welfare of the city and well-being of the whole of creation. It is, and must be, of public relevance.[4]

2. Benne, *Paradoxical Vision*.
3. Moltmann, *God for a Secular Society*.
4. All quotes in this paragraph are from the Contemporary English Version (CEV).

INTERRUPTION AND IMAGINATION

Considering the public character of theology David Tracy speaks of three different publics of theology: church, academy, and society.[5] The church is the community of religious faith, the practice and discourse in which the theologian is embedded. In this context theology seeks to critically clarify the contents and implications of the Christian faith and the faith of the church. The academy, on the other hand, is the sphere where theology presents itself to, and is questioned by, other academic disciplines and their assumptions, perspectives, and insights. As an academic discipline theology can be defined as systematic, methodical, and critical work with the aim of producing new theological knowledge and understanding. This provides a starting point for comparing theological inquiry with other academic activities, but is also a framework for discussing the relationship between various academic fields and requires that the theologian is loyal to the methodological and ethical principles of academic inquiry. As Tracy puts it in *Blessed Rage for Order*:

> In principle, the fundamental loyalty of the theologian *qua* theologian is to that morality of scientific knowledge which he shares with his colleagues, the philosophers, historians, and social scientists. No more than they, can he allow his own—or his tradition's—beliefs to serve as warrant for his arguments. In fact, in all proper theological inquiry, the analysis should be characterized by those same ethical stances of autonomous judgement, critical reflection, and properly skeptical hard-mindedness that characterize analysis in other fields. (. . .) the theologian finds that this basic faith, his fundamental attitude towards reality, is the same faith shared implicitly or explicitly by his secular contemporaries.[6]

A typology suggested by Hans Frei is helpful in distinguishing different ways of relating academic theology and philosophy to theology as an internal church activity and self-description.[7] Frei's first category sees theology primarily as an academic and philosophical discipline, with Immanuel Kant as an illustrative example. The perspective is external, academic, and philosophical, with a focus on meaningfulness, coherency, and logic. The second kind of theology seeks to correlate to what are specifically Christian with general cultural meaning structures, for example along the lines of Rudolf Bultmann's use of existentialism to understand theology.

---

5. Tracy, *Analogical Imagination*.
6. Tracy, *Blessed Rage for Order*, 7–8.
7. Frei, Hunsinger, and Placher, *Types of Christian Theology*. See also Ford, *Theology*.

Thirdly, Frei identifies a separate kind of theology in attempts to correlate Christian theology to the world, but not relying on a specific philosophy. He places Friedrich Schleiermacher in this category. The fourth category puts a stronger emphasis on what is specifically Christian, but remains open towards society and cultural context. Here Karl Barth is mentioned as a typical exponent. Lastly, the fifth type of theology is a kind of theology that rejects any association with the social context of theology. In this kind of theology the Christian self-understanding is emphasized through the reading of the Bible and Christian tradition. Theology is undertaken purely from the internal perspective of the Christian community. Frei places the works of D. Z. Phillips within this category. Public theology's theological identity combined with a commitment to society at large seems to indicate that public theology must avoid the extremes in this typology and find its shape and form within the three middle categories identified.

Tracy's third public of theology is society. This is the context where theology and Christian faith present themselves to a wider public and to contemporary culture. To Tracy this implies an obligation to speak in the public and "in a manner that can be disclosive and transformative for any intelligent, reasonable, responsible human being."[8] The relationship between Christian theology and this cultural context can be conceived of in different ways, and in a classic study Richard Niebuhr outlines five models: Christ against culture, Christ of culture, Christ above culture, Christ and culture in paradox, and Christ the transformer of culture.[9] The first model—Christ against culture—is the most uncompromising view of culture. Loyalty to the authority of Christ is combined with rejection of cultural society, and a clear line of separation is drawn between the two. The second model—Christ of culture—does not see the same tension between Christ and culture. Rather, they interpret each other and Jesus is hailed as "the fulfiller of society's hopes and aspirations."[10] The third model—Christ above culture—sees culture as neither good nor bad, but problematic. Niebuhr finds that those who hold this position:

> cannot separate works of human culture from the grace of God, for all those works are possible only by grace. But neither can they separate the experience of grace from cultural activity; for how

---

8. Tracy, "Defending," 351.
9. Niebuhr, *Christ and Culture*.
10. Ibid., 83.

can men love the unseen God in response to his love without serving the visible brother in human society?[11]

The fourth model—Christ and culture in paradox—also wants to combine Christ and culture, but finds this much more difficult than in the Christ above culture-model given the parallel existence of sin and grace in culture. Finally, the fifth model—Christ the transformer of Culture—represents the more optimistic attitude towards culture. God is seen as interacting with men and women in historical human events and it is assumed that human culture can be "a transformed human life in and to the glory of God."[12]

While Niebuhr seems to have a preference for the latter—the Christian transformation of culture-model—Miroslav Volf is critical of any assimilation of contemporary culture and favors a multidimensional understanding of the Christ and culture-relationship. He finds that Christian identity is:

> always a complex and flexible network of small and large refusals, divergences, subversions, and more or less radical and encompassing alternative proposals and enactments, surrounded by the acceptance of many cultural givens. There is no single way to relate to a given culture as a whole or even to its dominant thrust; there are only numerous ways of accepting, transforming, or replacing various aspects of a given culture from within.[13]

In this perspective, public theology is challenged to be part of the culture and to criticize the culture. It is challenged to provoke and protest, but also to seek to include, negotiate, and reconcile.

Max L. Stackhouse and Elaine Graham add to Tracy's distinction between church, academy, and society by identifying the market as a fourth public for theology.[14] Sebastian Kim has suggested an even more detailed categorization, distinguishing between six categories or main bodies engaged in the public sphere. These are the state (politics, policy-making, public sector), market (economics, business), civil society (non-governmental organizations, interest groups), academies (higher education institutions), religious communities (institutionalized religions, congregations), and the media (broadcasting, publications, internet). Kim argues these are "common to all modern societies but the relative power of each and the

---

11. Ibid., 119.
12. Ibid., 196.
13. Volf, *A Public Faith*, 93.
14. Graham, *Between a Rock and a Hard Place*, 84.

interrelations between them may vary from one society to another,"[15] thus reminding us of the contextual and historical character of the public sphere at any given time or place.

Since the Christian faith is inherently public and theology is a public undertaking, it is the dedicated task of public theology to clarify and manifest the meaning and implications of this faith in the public sphere in relation to all these different publics, and taking into account the diverse issues of public concern and interest. Along these lines Graham identifies three convictions of public theology: Firstly, religion is more than a personal or private matter, but "carries over into the believer's life in all aspects of the public domain."[16] Secondly, and following from the first, religion has a public significance. On this point Graham quotes Stackhouse who finds that theology "is an argument regarding the way things are and ought to be, one decisive for public discourse and necessary to the guidance of individual souls, societies, and, indeed, the community of nations."[17] Thirdly, "theology must be a fully public, dialogical discourse, in terms of being prepared to defend its core principles *in public*."[18]

The multitude of publics implies, however, that glocal public theology is not only part of, but needs to relate to, several different audiences and constituencies. In addition, public theology needs to acknowledge the wider context for these publics, i.e., the post-modern and post-secular character of contemporary society and the precarious lives many people live. This implies that there is room and opportunity for churches and Christians to participate in and contribute to the public sphere, but it does not mean that the public sphere is in fact an open, inclusive sphere in the Habermasian sense. Public theology must acknowledge that even in today's multicultural, pluralist, post-modern, and post-secular societies, participation is not the privilege of all. Power and privilege are not equally distributed and constitute a profound challenge to concerned citizens, churches, and public theology.

---

15. Kim, *Theology in the Public Sphere*, 12.

16. Graham, *Between a Rock and a Hard Place*, xxiii.

17. Stackhouse, "Public Theology and Ethical Judgement," 165, quoted in Graham, *Between a Rock and a Hard Place*, xxiii.

18. Graham, *Between a Rock and a Hard Place*, xxiii, original emphasis.

INTERRUPTION AND IMAGINATION

THE HISTORY AND CRITICISM OF PUBLIC THEOLOGY

These challenges found in the relationship between Christian faith and theology on the one hand, and culture, wider society, and the public sphere on the other hand, are not new. Christian contributions to public debates and social and political issues have a long history. In fact, it is already reflected in Jesus' call to "Give the Emperor what belongs to him and give God what belongs to God" (Matt 22:21)[19] and in Paul's analysis in Rom 13. The relationship between the Christian church and political authorities has, for historical, political, and ecclesiastical reasons, been necessary to think through ever since Constantin's decision to make Christianity the state religion of the Roman Empire, as in for example Augustin's *The City of God*.[20] Similarly, Martin Luther's doctrine of two kingdoms (or governments) interpreted the relationship between the church and secular authorities in the sixteenth century, and is widely referred to even in contemporary debates on religion and politics, church and state, etc.

Closer to the present day, liberal Protestantism was a nineteenth-century expression of a Christian commitment to social reform and progress.[21] The related social gospel movement represented a Christian involvement in the social and political challenges of the times, with Walter Rauschenbusch as one of the movement's prime representatives.[22] He and others sought ways of making the Christian faith and gospel relevant in a period of deep socio-economic and political challenges, but was also quite optimistic about the possibilities for creating a better society. The relationship between Church and society was viewed with great optimism, relying on a harmonious understanding of the relationship between theology and culture as the basic premise of theology.

This optimism concerning contemporary culture and the political challenges and developments of the day so characteristic of liberal theology and the social gospel movement, received a strong blow with the First World War and in the trenches of Northern France. Karl Barth and Dietrich Bonhoeffer then became key representatives of a new theological skepticism to culture and social life in theological terms. This skepticism led,

---

19. Contemporary English Version (CEV).
20. Augustine, *Confessions*.
21. Herrmann, *Ethik*.
22. Rauschenbusch, *Theology for the Social Gospel*.

however, not to a withdrawal from society, but to a powerful engagement with the political and economic developments of their time.

Nazism and fascism soon became another significant challenge to Christians, theologians, and churches (and many others). German churches were Nazified, but a resistance church, the Church of the confessing Christians (*die Bekenntniskirche*) was also established. Consequently, the Church became deeply divided. In theological literature this has become known as *status confessionis*—a situation of confessional-character. This means that the Church is divided in its response to a question that touches upon the very foundations of the ecclesiastical community.

Barth and Bonhoeffer were both central in the Church's struggle against Nazism and Paul Tillich and Reinhold Niebuhr are two further examples of theologians who engaged in social criticism. Nazism caused Tillich to flee to the United States where he and Reinhold Niebuhr developed a critical theology and social analysis. This social analysis was, however, explicitly theologically informed, rooted in, and shaped by a conversation with the Christian tradition. In this sense they all exercised a form of theological social analysis.

After WWII the ecumenical movement grew stronger and several initiatives were taken to find a new and stronger role for churches in the reconstruction after the war, and thus a role in the political arena both nationally and internationally. This inspired another reaction against liberal theology and the development of what has been called ecumenical social ethics. This was influenced by the Christian realism of Reinhold Niebuhr and the related middle axiom approach of J. H. Oldham in the United Kingdom. Niebuhr argued that liberal theology had been overly optimistic and naive in its approach to social concerns and political problems. In particular, he argued that sin was unavoidable, and that society therefore would always be an immoral society. Men (and women) could be able of acting in a loving and benevolent way, but not in the political realm to an extent that could change this basic feature of social life.[23]

Since then, all of these approaches have been criticized. One criticism is that this kind of public theology relies extensively on immanent human reasoning and our ability to address and deal with social concerns. In other words, public theology shares not only the optimism of liberal theology, but also retains its naivety. A related criticism comes from scholars who are deeply skeptical about the defining secular features of the public sphere

---

23. Niebuhr, *Moral Man and Immoral Society*.

and thus reject any participation in it on such premises. Public theology is seen as an undertaking that puts Christianity in the service of institutions, groups, and powers foreign to, and often opposed to, the Christian tradition. Representatives of radical orthodoxy such as Stanley Hauerwas and John Milbank in particular have voiced this kind of criticism.[24] Although Hauerwas believes the Christian faith and Christians can make a unique contribution to public policy formation, his political contribution is primarily critical rather than constructive. Hauerwas tends to see Niebuhrian public theology as a way of "compromise, accommodation, and finally unfaithfulness"[25] and it is this kind of criticism that makes Charles Mathewes write a theology of public life rather than public theology. He claims public theologies typically "are self-destructive accommodationist: they let the "larger" secular world's self-understanding set the terms, and then ask how religious faith contributes to the purposes of public life, so understood."[26]

Despite his criticism of public theology, Hauerwas can also be seen as an important contributor to the field. As Robert Benne points out:

> His emphases on the church as a community of character, on a virtue ethic, and particularly on the story of Jesus as the key source of Christian formation have served to recall Protestants to the Bible and the church as the guiding beacons for Christian existence in the world. (. . .) So, while on one level Hauerwas seems to eschew the task of public theology, on another he has helped the Protestant mainstream regain an authentically Christian—rather than a political or psychological—voice by which to address the public world.[27]

Although these differences could be interpreted as "illuminating and complementary of one another,"[28] it seems to me that Hauerwas and others in the same tradition are too critical and too suspicious about society at large and the public sphere. Where Hauerwas finds the public debate solely governed and controlled by forces external to the church, not least the state, it seems to me that public theology cannot give up the task and challenge of theological engagement in the public sphere. Not only as citizens and part

---

24. Hauerwas, *After Christendom?* and Milbank, *Theology and Social Theory*.
25. True, "Embracing Hauerwas?," 209.
26. Mathewes, *Theology of Public Life*, 1.
27. Benne, *Paradoxical Vision*, 44–45.
28. True, "Embracing Hauerwas?," 209.

of civil society, but also as churches and Christians, we have a responsibility to participate in public discussions and the processes of actual political decision making.

Another reaction against ecumenical social ethics came from the global South and in the form of a much more radical theological approach: liberation theology. Later this was itself challenged by the end of the cold war and with the assumed victory of capitalism and the West and thus the end of history.[29] However, resistance against social, economic, and political injustice and oppression persists, and liberation theology lives on, although in other forms and with different kinds of emphasis than the kind that gave it its name in the first place.

THE SOCIAL LOCATION OF PUBLIC THEOLOGY

The modern field of public theology has developed as part of, and in opposition to, these theological developments. The contemporary scholarly field of public theology is commonly traced back to Martin Marty's use of the term in his discussion of Niebuhr and is closely linked to Christian realism.[30] Since then, a growing literature on theology and public issues has emerged and been regarded as contributions to public theology. Several have come from the North American context: David Tracy, John Courtney Murray, Reinholdt Niebuhr, Ronald F. Thiemann, Robert Benne, Max L. Stackhouse, Miroslav Volf, and many others.[31]

In the United Kingdom, William Temple's *Christianity and Social Order*[32] is a modern classic. In Temple's footsteps J. H. Oldham, John Atherton, Ronald H. Preston, Duncan B. Forrester, and William F. Storrar[33] have made important contributions, as have Sebastian Kim, Rowan Williams, and Elaine Graham.[34] In continental Europe, the field of public theology

---

29. Fukuyama, *End of History*.

30. Marty, "Two Kinds."

31. See Niebuhr, *Moral Man and Immoral Society*; Tracy, *Analogical Imagination*; Thiemann, *Constructing a Public Theology*; Murray, *We Hold These Truths*; Stackhouse, *God and Globalization*; Hainsworth and Paeth, *Public Theology*; Volf, *A Public Faith* and Paeth, Breitenberg, and Lee, *Shaping Public Theology*.

32. Temple, *Christianity and Social Order*.

33. See Preston, *Church and Society*; Preston, *Religion*; Forrester, *Christian Justice*; Atherton, *Public Theology*; Forrester, *Truthful Action*; and Storrar and Morton, *Public Theology*.

34. See Kim, *Theology in the Public Sphere*; Williams, *Faith in the Public Square*; and Graham, *Between a Rock and a Hard Place*.

has been developed in particular by the German theologians Wolfgang Huber and Heinrich Bedford-Strohm.[35] Another important center for public theology is South Africa, with roots in the resistance against apartheid but more explicitly developed as public theology in the post-apartheid period. Important contributions have come from John W. de Gruchy, Nico Koopman, and others.[36] In addition, there are of course scholars in other parts of the world who have contributed to the field, including scholars in Australia, New Zealand, Latin America, and others.

In terms of denominational affiliation, many of the contributions to public theology have come from Protestant scholars. Adam Kuyper, Max L. Stackhouse, and others have had a Reformed approach in their work, as is the case with the work of Duncan B. Forrester and William F. Storrar. A public theology with a stronger Lutheran character has been developed and articulated in Ronald F. Thiemann's *Constructing a Public Theology*[37] and Robert Benne's *The Paradoxical Vision*.[38] More recently, the Lutheran contribution to public theology is discussed further in a *Festschrift* in honor of the Benne[39] and in Bedford-Strohm's several articles in the field.[40] Contributions addressing Catholic social teaching have not to the same extent been explicitly linked to public theology, but are nevertheless highly relevant to the field.[41] Today, however, public theology is to a large extent developed through international and inter-denominational discussions.

The expansion of public theology from the North to countries in the global South as well as the influx in the sheer number of publications in the field reflects a redistribution of power, focus, and attention from the

---

35. See Huber, *Kirche Und Öffentlichkeit*; Bedford-Strohm, "Public Theology and the Global Economy"; Bedford-Strohm, "Poverty and Public Theology"; and Bedford-Strohm, "Public Theology and Political Ethics."

36. See De Gruchy, "From Political to Public Theologies"; De Gruchy, "Public Theology"; Smit, *Essays in Public Theology*; Koopman, "Public Theology in (South) Africa"; Koopman, "Public Theology as Prophetic Theology"; Koopman, "Some Contours for Public Theology" and Koopman, "Churches and Public Policy."

37. Thiemann, *Constructing a Public Theology*.

38. Benne, *Paradoxical Vision*.

39. Shahan, *Report from the Front Lines*.

40. These include Bedford-Strohm, "Public Theology and the Global Economy"; Bedford-Strohm, "Public Theology of Ecology"; and Bedford-Strohm, "Public Theology and Political Ethics."

41. See Murray, *We Hold These Truths* and Hollenbach, *Common Good*.

center to the periphery. Mario I. Aguilar describes this as re-invention, re-location, and re-subjection:

> Two processes seem to permeate the taxonomic possibilities of the complexity of public theology: re-invention and re-location. By re-inventing public theologies new subjects of theologizing and new themes arise, according to the ongoing changes of society and the globalized community. By a natural process of re-location public theology tends to regroup with ecclesial structures and to re-assess possible locations for the subjects of theologizing. Both processes are plausible and theologically agreeable. However, my own preference is for a process of re-subjection, of change and exchange of the role of the theologian and the possibilities of creating narratives about God (theology) within a globalized community and particularly within the centers of Christianity located in Latin America, Africa and Asia.[42]

This development should be welcomed. In the same way that the public sphere is an open, cross-cultural arena, public theology should be located, rooted, and shaped by more than middle-class, Western academics. Participation by all is an ideal not only in the public sphere, but also in the field of public theology. Public theology should be an inherently discursive, dialogic, participatory theology. This broad participation should, however, not be taken for granted. As Storrar has pointed out:

> it is the continuing pastoral task of public theology in the public sphere; through story and lament, through critical social analysis and theological reflection, giving constructive and healing expression to the public anger of the many different silenced and excluded voices of the oppressed or the marginalized.[43]

To Storrar, it is "the responsibility of public theology (. . .) to help to create and sustain such public forums, as well as to participate in them."[44] In other words, public theology must protect and promote the public sphere. Public theology has "a bias for inclusivity"[45] and must seek to promote the participation of everyone in the public sphere. In this sense, public theology can be described as a "theology of witness"[46]—a witness of the margin-

---

42. Aguilar, "Public Theology," 325.
43. Storrar, "Naming of Parts," 31.
44. Ibid., 34–35.
45. Atherton, "Marginalisation," 29.
46. De Gruchy, "From Political to Public Theologies," 46.

alized and oppressed on the underside of history and outside globalization, as well as a witness of Christian faith and conviction.

MODELS OF PUBLIC THEOLOGY

With this history and multiple social locations it is not surprising that public theology comes in different forms. Breitenberg distinguishes between three types of public theology.[47] Firstly, there is a descriptive and analytical approach to public theology. This approach is found primarily in academic public theology and focusses on how theologians, churches, clergy, and lay Christians in the past and present have acted as public theologians or offered models or theories for the practice and study of public theology. The field is concerned with identifying the common characteristics and interests of public theology.

Secondly, there is a more constructive and normative way of working with public theology. This kind of public theology deals with the ongoing discussions about how public theology should be practiced and the field of study understood. Public theology of this kind thus deals with both what public theologians do and the question of how public theology should be carried out.

The third approach is equally constructive, but also more applied than the second. This is the "theologically grounded and informed interpretations of and guidance for institutions, interactions, events, circumstances, policies, and practices, both within and outside the church."[48] This refers to the work done on substantive issues that are (or should be) of concern to the Church and/or "the larger society." Some scholars, practical-public theologians such as Robert Benne, Max L. Stackhouse, Ronald F. Thiemann, and Rowan Williams have contributed to all of these dimensions of public theology.

Stackhouse too distinguishes between three competing models of public theology. He names them the confessional, dogmatic, and apologetic models.[49] The confessional model relies strongly on the particular

---

47. Breitenberg, "To Tell the Truth."

48. Ibid., 64.

49. Stackhouse also distinguishes between the dogmatic, polemical and apologetic modes of theology (Stackhouse, "Public Theology and Ethical Judgement") and between confessional, contextual, dogmatic and apologetic theologies (Stackhouse, *God and Globalization*, 4:105–7).

perspective of Christian theology or even a specific denomination within this tradition. In addition it "understands each faith as highly particular and basically not accessible to any who do not believe it."[50] This is not the model Stackhouse advocates and Breitenberg similarly argues that public theology "stands in contrast to those exclusively confessional theologies that do not intentionally and explicitly seek to provide interpretations of and guidance for society's public sectors, institutions, and interactions, as a primary end of the church."[51]

The dogmatic model offers a social-ethical doctrine based on its own presuppositions, similar to a "party platform or manifesto." However, "[a]lthough it knows that its deepest views are not universally shared, it proclaims these dogmas in public forums as it seeks to influence public consciousness and public policy in a desired direction."[52] The model Stackhouse favors is the apologetic model. This is the stronger form of public theology and "claims that the deepest assumptions of faith are, and can be shown to be, as reasonable, as ethical and as viable for an authentic, warranted commitment as any other known religion or philosophy and, indeed, indispensable to other modes of public discourse."[53]

This apologetic dimension of public theology is retained in what Graham presents as a post-secular public theology. She draws on Stackhouse's "insistence that public theology necessarily involves an apologetic function, in that it must always be prepared to 'give an account' of its motives and values in a way that is accessible to its interlocutors."[54] Graham develops three motifs of what she calls post-secular public theology, incorporating several of the concerns of public theology outlined above:

> First, public theology as Christian apologetics, above all, is concerned primarily with 'the welfare of the city where I have sent you into exile, and pray to the Lord on its behalf, for in its welfare you will find your welfare' (Jeremiah 29.7 NRSV).
>
> Second in keeping with the early Christian apologists who regarded their defences of faith as petitions to the rulers, I consider what it means to promote public theology as 'speaking truth to power'. This renews the historic commitment of public theologians

---

50. Stackhouse, "Public Theology and Political Economy," 191.
51. Breitenberg, "To Tell the Truth," 66.
52. Stackhouse, "Public Theology and Political Economy," 191.
53. Ibid., 191.
54. Graham, *Between a Rock and a Hard Place*, 211.

to serve as advocates and speak prophetically into structures and institutions in the name of justice.

As my third motif, then, continuing that of an apologetics of praxis and presence, I want to advance a plea for greater attention to a neglected aspect of public theology: the secular vocation and formation of the laity. It summons the institutional Church to take very seriously the business of fostering a deeper and more extensive theological literacy among the laity. This returns us to the relationship between words and actions in apologetics: while the practices of faithful citizenship constitute a kind of first-order public theology, they may still need justification. 'Giving an account of oneself' may be expressed in the praxis of care, social activism, and active citizenship, but it must also mean being able to speak with conviction into a reasoned public debate.[55]

To Graham, Christian apologetics of this kind offers the opportunity to reclaim "notions of theology as a form of practical wisdom—theology as the discourse of faith that facilitates faithful discipleship; and public theology in particular, as articulating that in relation to the liminal space between private and public, sacred and secular, Church and world."[56] Her use of the term apologetics must, in other words, be understood in line with a model of apologetics "that commends the 'truth' not as correspondence with propositional knowledge but as exemplary lifestyle, as a world into which another is invited, in the understanding that cultural context conditions a response."[57]

GLOCALLY ENGAGED PUBLIC THEOLOGY

All of these approaches share the conviction that public theology is an articulation of a Christian faith—a faith which is global in at least two ways: 1) Christians around the world confess their Christian faith and interpret it in multiple different ways, and 2) this Christian faith is a faith in one God, creator of every human being, heaven and earth. At the same time, public theology is closely related to the particular contexts and situations the practitioners of public theology find themselves in. In this sense, public

---

55. Ibid., 213.
56. Ibid., 181.
57. Ibid., 204.

theology can also be understood and articulated as expressions of ordinary theology,[58] people's theology[59] or contextual theology.[60]

As such particular theologies travel across social, cultural, ethnic, and religious divides they are made accessible to a wider audience in the public sphere. In effect, they become shared between rich and poor, the privileged and non-privileged, the North and South, East and West. Interpretations and viewpoints developed from different local settings and perspectives meet, potentially leading to new insights, approaches, and theological understanding. As noted, the local and global are not opposites but interrelated. Today's age of globalization is therefore not the end of contextual theologies.

The same applies to public theology. In local congregations and churches, amongst Christians of one denominational character or ecumenically between Christians of different denominations, contextual theologies are being developed. When these theologies are given a public expression in the form of worship, public statements, political campaigning etc., they also become examples of public theology: theological statements in the public sphere, local and global at the same time. This is not only a descriptive claim, but also a normative one. Public theology should combine the particular with the universal. It needs to be *glocal*.[61]

In addition, public theology needs to focus on social affairs. The plight and suffering in the world gives public theology a normative agenda. It needs to be a contextually engaged theology. As Michael S. Hogue points out, "the tasks of critique, clarification, and normative negotiation occur outside of the religious community proper and in relation to the broader sociocultural conditions, processes, spheres, and political and moral challenges of human life."[62] Hogue's normative understanding of public theology differs, however, from for example that of Stackhouse. Hogue finds that Stackhouse's approach amounts to a form of unilateral correlationalism with a strong normative thrust and apologetic shape, and he argues that while Stackhouse's "quest for the singularly normative may be partly built into received forms of theological apologetic, it betrays an insufficient regard for the reflexivity that is both generated by and needs to be

---

58. Astley and Francis, *Exploring Ordinary Theology*.
59. Amirtham and Pobee, *Theology by the People*.
60. Bevans, *Models of Contextual Theology* and Bergmann, *God in Context*.
61. Pearson, "Quest for a Glocal Public Theology."
62. Hogue, "After the Secular," 353.

cooperatively facilitated in a pluralistic time of global moral challenges."[63] As an alternative to Stackhouse's apologetic approach he therefore suggests a pragmatic public theology. This he defines as

> an inter-traditional public theological mode that is methodologically fallibilized, doxologically rather than apologetically focused, strategically engaged *in medias res* between traditions and global and local moral challenges, and normatively committed to the nurturance of differentiated moral solidarities with and on behalf of the most vulnerable.[64]

Hogue argues this pragmatic approach takes more fully into account globalization's radical transformations of contemporary religiosities. He argues that "insofar as pragmatic public theology is shaped by commitments to participative listening and solidary contextual analysis, then normative aspirations emerge through a collaborative hermeneutic rather than being articulated upfront and unilaterally."[65] This would make pragmatic theology "unapologetically *partial* in its methodological as well as normative commitments to interpreting and responding to moral challenges with those individuals and communities whose lives are being most directly formed and deformed by them."[66]

In this way, Houge seems to incorporate a liberationist option for the poor in his otherwise pragmatic approach to public theology. The Christian character of public theology seems, however, to be weakened. The former comes across as the strength of Hogue's pragmatic approach, while the latter seems to undermine the distinct character of public theology as *theologically* informed contributions to the public sphere.

POLITICAL AND LIBERATION THEOLOGY

A wide range of hyphenated theologies bear witness to the close relationship between Christian theology and the context with in which they are articulated: African theology, Latin American theology, black, feminist, queer theology etc. In addition, there is political theology, indigenous theology, liberation theology, secular theology, eco-theology, and many more.

63. Ibid., 366.
64. Ibid., 346, original emphasis.
65. Ibid., 368.
66. Ibid., 369, original emphasis.

Public Theology

Public theology relates to several of these in many different ways. In the following I want to highlight two of them: political theology and liberation theology.[67]

The roots of modern political theology are often traced back to the works of the German scholar Carl Schmitt[68] whose contributions are tainted by his authoritarian theories, sympathies with totalitarianism, and involvement with the Nazi regime. He did, however, discuss the relationship between liberal ideology and secularism, and used religious resources to articulate an alternative approach to the status quo. For this reason Schmitt's analysis of theology, power, and political authority continues to be a reference point in the field.

Schmitt's legacy has caused political theology to be referred to "theologies in Europe that gave legitimacy to the state and its claims within the context of Christendom."[69] Other scholars have, however, developed political theology in a quite different direction, focusing more on the relationship between Christian theology and politics, ethics, and religion.[70] In the 1960s, with Johann Baptist Metz and Jürgen Moltmann, political theology shifted from a discussion of the theological dimension of politics to the political aspects of theology. Metz discussed the concept of political theology using a Marxist approach,[71] while Moltmann saw political theology as dealing with "the political consciousness of theology itself."[72] Today, the journal *Political Theology* "investigates the connections religious and political issues and practices" aiming to "examine the explicit or implicit religious background to political movements, ideas, and practices; examine the political implications of religious movements, ideas, and practices;

---

67. Here I follow Sebastian Kim who contrasts public theology with its two close relatives political theology and liberation theology. He also provides instructive tables that give a good overview over their differences and similarities in terms of context, main theologians, issues, theological themes, methodology, aim, and limitation/criticism. See Kim, *Theology in the Public Sphere*, 23–24.

68. Schmitt, *Political Theology*.

69. De Gruchy, "From Political to Public Theologies," 47.

70. Examples include Reinhold Niebuhr (*Moral Man*), Johann Baptist Metz (*Faith in History*), Oliver O'Donovan (*Desire of the Nations*), Nicholas Wolterstorff (*Mighty and the Almighty*), and many others.

71. Metz, *Passion for God*.

72. Moltmann, "Political Theology," 6.

[and] interrogate the way power operates at the intersection of religion and politics."[73]

Political theology has thus become an increasingly diversified field, though two primary categories can be identified. The first has a distinct philosophical character and can be found in the field of critical humanities. Scholars in this category tend to question hegemonic ideas and interests with the aim of disclosing them and challenging the ideology, ruling interests, and power relationships of contemporary society. The other category is the kind of political theology that more explicitly draws on, and is informed by, theology. Often this is Christian theology, although examples of Jewish or Islamic political theology can also be found. While classic political theology is concerned with the theological foundations for state formation and civil authority, these kinds of political theology address policy making and the concerns and choices political authorities are faced with.[74]

Consequently, contemporary political theology gives special attention to political and socio-economic issues. Scholars in the field focus on the political relevance of theology to political process and political decision making. Accordingly, contributions in the field often make use of *policy discourse* and recommend particular choices and actions that can, and should be, done by persons with political responsibilities.[75] This policy dimension can also be found in public theology. Indeed, public theology is often a kind of political theology in that it addresses political issues discussed in the public sphere.

Indeed, as noted by Moltmann in the preface of *God for a Secular Society*, there are close connections between political theology and Christian public theology. He writes:

> Its subject alone necessarily makes Christian theology a *theologia publica*, public theology. It gets involved in the public affairs of society. It thinks about what is of general concern in the light of hope in Christ for the kingdom of God. It becomes political in the name of the poor and the marginalized in a given society. Remembrance of the crucified Christ makes it critical towards political religions

---

73. www.politicaltheology.com.

74. For more on the field of political theology, see Scott and Cavanaugh, *Blackwell Companion*; Vries and Sullivan, *Political Theologies*; Lilla, *Stillborn God*; Kirwan, *Political Theology*; Losonczi, Luoma-Aho, and Singh, *Future of Political Theology*; Critchley, *Faith of the Faithless*; Hovey, Cavanaugh, and Bailey, *Eerdmans Reader*; Phillips, *Political Theology*; Kessler, *Political Theology*; and Fiorenza, Tanner, and Welker, *Political Theology*.

75. Gustafson, "Varieties of Moral Discourse," 71–72.

and idolatries. It thinks critically about the religious and moral values of the societies in which it exists, and presents its reflections as a reasoned position.[76]

These connections and similarities between political and public theology do not, however, eliminate their differences. As noted by Bedford-Strohm:

> While there is also a close kinship to political theology, public theology makes clearer than political theology that the witness of the Gospel in the political realm can never be simply identified with a certain political programme. Even though there are clear ethical guidelines in the biblical material, such as the option for the poor, there must be a continuous open political discourse about the best ways to translate it into government policies.[77]

Against this background, it seems reasonable to regard political theology as a more specific and narrow concept than public theology. Public theology's emphasis is on participation in the public sphere, while political theology focuses on political structures, power, and decision making. Through participating in public debates, however, public theology also seeks to be publicly relevant, including with regard to policy and decision making.

Liberation theology traces its roots to Latin America and the 1960s. Gustavo Gutierrez published his book *A Theology of Liberation* in 1971 and presented in it the key features of a new way of thinking about and doing theology.[78] Later liberation theology found new expressions in other parts of the world responding to other contextual challenges. North American black theology[79] and feminist theology[80] share important traits with Latin American liberation theology and have expanded the scope of this theological approach profoundly. Accordingly, liberationist theology has also

---

76. Moltmann, *God for a Secular Society*, 1.

77. Bedford-Strohm, "Public Theology and Political Ethics," 291.

78. Gutiérrez, *Theology of Liberation*. Introductions to liberation theology can be found in Boff and Boff, *Introducing Liberation Theology*; Rowland, *Cambridge Companion*, and Cooper, *Reemergence of Liberation Theologies*. The social and historical background of liberation theology is discussed by Enrique Dussel ("The Sociohistorical Meaning") and even more elaborate by Christian Smith (*Emergence of Liberation Theology*). More recent contributions within liberationist political theology include Rieger, *Opting for the Margins*; Petrella, *Future of Liberation Theology*; Petrella, *Beyond Liberation Theology*; and Cooper, *Reemergence of Liberation Theologies*.

79. Cone, *Black Theology of Liberation*.

80. Ruether, *Sexism and God-Talk*.

INTERRUPTION AND IMAGINATION

been developed through a wide range of contributions from scholars from all continents and denominations. With the end of the Cold war and liberalism's assumed victory over Marxism, liberation theology was dismissed and declared dead. As noted, however, liberation theology remains an important source for critical social analysis and a spiritual inspiration to churches and Christians world-wide. Despite external criticism and internal controversies,[81] this approach to theology and society continues to be reclaimed and reinvented as it finds new contextual expressions.

Liberation theology also goes under the name of prophetic theology. As such, it takes its name from the visionary prophets who announce a future qualitatively different from the present and a vision for social change. Prophetic theology is characterized by its critical and utopian aspects, often with a strong emphasis on liberation and justice. Typically, the criticism addresses root causes to problems in society. The language is symbolic and metaphorical, and "moves us from indignation with the present to aspiration for the future."[82]

Regarding the relationship between liberation theology and public theology, this too is disputed. Robert J. Schreiter has suggested that the task of liberation theology should include not only resistance, denunciation, and critique, but also advocacy and reconstruction.[83] This would bring liberation theology closer to public theology, and Bedford-Strohm has indeed argued that "public theology is liberation theology for a democratic society."[84] Storrar, on the other hand, places theologies that represent what he calls "public anger"[85] outside public theology, but this has been criticized by for example South African James R. Cochrane.[86]

In the following I will consider public theology as a category wider than liberation theology and hold that the latter on the whole tends to rely on a more exclusive radical social analysis than that which is often the case within public theology. Still, the emphasis on liberation and justice as well as the vision for social change is an important liberationist dimension of public theology. Public theology too is committed to the preferential option

---

81. McGovern, *Liberation Theology*.
82. Koopman, "Public Theology as Prophetic Theology," 121.
83. Schreiter, *New Catholicity*, 109–10.
84. Bedford-Strohm, "Public Theology and Political Ethics," 291.
85. Storrar, "Naming of Parts," 31.
86. Cochrane, "Against the Grain."

Public Theology

for the poor highlighted by liberation theology and this provides a normative starting point when approaching social and political issues.

THE PARADOXICAL VISION

Most contributions to public theology deal with specific issues rather than the identity and understanding of public theology per se. Graham's *Between a Rock and a Hard Place* is a recent and important exception where she discusses a public theology for the post-secular age.[87] Another exception is Benne's *The Paradoxical Vision* where he outlines a public theology for the twenty-first century.[88] Although he draws heavily on Lutheran perspectives, Benne outlines a framework for public theology that is worthwhile considering even beyond his denominational home ground.

Benne's framework for public theology comprises of four themes or principles that both relate to one another and overlap. These are 1) the qualitative distinction between God's salvation and all human efforts, 2) the paradox of human nature, 3) God's paradoxical rule, and 4) the paradox of history. The first of these refers to the notion that "the saving work of God in Christ is totally the work of God. Before God with regard to their salvation, humans are purely receptive. God's redemption is a gift, pure and simple."[89] Benne denies that this leads to political quietism or cynicism, but argues:

> Liberated from worry about our salvation, we can turn unobsessively to the human task of building a better world, not by prideful claims of transformation, but by determined yet humble attempts to make small steps for the better.
>
> Certainly this relativization of human efforts does not make them unimportant for Christians. The Christian response to God's grace is faith toward God and love toward one's neighbor. Faith and love go together. In this sense, faith without works is indeed dead. So obedience follows faith; it is not the route to salvation, but rather its result.[90]

The second principle refers to the Lutheran doctrine of the Christian as *simul justus et peccator*, simultaneously justified and sinner. Benne holds

---

87. Graham, *Between a Rock and a Hard Place*.
88. Benne, *Paradoxical Vision*.
89. Ibid., 69.
90. Ibid., 72.

that humans are irretrievably committed to finding something other than God to which to fasten their hearts. This is the inescapable sin of our lives. But, as Benne puts it:

> humans are not dirt. Even in their fallen state they possess qualities of their creation in the image of God. (. . .) Indeed, our rationality, though fallen, can help us to discern what is right and just behavior with regard to our fellow human beings. We are capable of "civil righteousness."[91]

The third principle, God's paradoxical rule, refers to another hallmark of Lutheran theology: the doctrine of two kingdoms or the twofold rule of God. This has been misinterpreted and misused to advocate a separation between church and state, salvation and social life, the secular world and the life of the church. Consequently, Lutherans (and others) have committed themselves to political quietism. However, rather than a doctrine of dualism, this is a doctrine of duality. Benne argues "[w]e are caught in two realities that must be taken seriously."[92] God works in two ways in the world to confront and detain evil and sin: through worldly authorities to preserve social order, and through the church and its proclamation of the Gospel. In other words, phrased in terms of how Christianity relates to culture, this is a Christ and culture in paradox teaching. God rules in two ways in the world, amounting to a paradoxical twofold rule. This can also be expressed in the Lutheran distinction between Law and Gospel: "At the same time that God sustains the world through law, he also offers salvation through the gospel."[93]

Fourthly, there is the paradox of history. Although Jesus proclaimed that the Kingdom of God had arrived (Luke 17:21), he also warned that it is not of this world (John 18:36). Accordingly, we live in a time between the first coming of the Kingdom, and its coming in its fullness sometime in the future. Benne's key point in this connection is that "[h]umans in their finitude and sin cannot complete history. There is simply no room for utopian expectations in the paradoxical vision."[94] This does not, however, mean that Benne rules out historical improvements. There is hope, both in God's final victory and in history:

---

91. Ibid., 77.
92. Ibid., 80.
93. Ibid., 86.
94. Ibid., 89–90.

this judgment on human sin is only one side of the paradox, for God has also given us a hope. First, we have a hope that transcends history, the promise that God's love will finally be triumphant over all that resists it. (. . .) Second, we have the possibility of historical hope. God has given humans the capacity for civil righteousness. Because God's dynamic law of creation operates in the historical process, good things can happen. Improvements are possible, though certainly not guaranteed. Christians are obligated to participate in good efforts.[95]

This principle contrasts with views that see "God's redemptive actions run through all events" and according to which, "the kingdom of God can and will come in history."[96] Benne points out that both Catholic theology and Marxist inspired liberation theology embody similar problems. Benne writes:

> In Lutheran parlance, these tendencies violate the twofold rule of God by making the law into the gospel. The creative, sustaining, and judging actions of God are mistaken for the gospel, a mistake that distorts both law and gospel. Such an error loads too much onto worldly processes. Highly ambiguous realities are claimed to be salvific. At its worst, those "on the right side of history" claim God's saving power for their endeavors.[97]

Another problem Benne is concerned about is the inverse: that the gospel is made into law. He argues:

> Instead of making human activity into the salvation of God (making the law into the gospel), the gospel, with its radical theme of agape love, is made into a law. The radical love that God shows humans in Christ becomes a direct principle for guiding life in the public world. Further, the intense personal responses to the gospel—faith, love, and hope—are directly applied to the ambiguities of the fallen world.[98]

Benne exemplifies this in the "constant drift toward pacifism. Forgiving love that underestimates the destructive intentions of the enemy, turning the other cheek, refusing to use coercive power against evil, unilateral

---

95. Ibid., 90.
96. Ibid., 91.
97. Ibid., 92.
98. Ibid., 94.

disarmament, and unilateral freezes of weapons development."[99] Benne finds that this amounts to a kind of sentimentalism in the Christian, Reformed tradition in particular:

> The problem with all this is that the "gospel ethic" is not fit for the challenges of the world. The cross reminds us of that. The world cannot be directly run by gospel love or the Christian virtues that are elicited by it. The world is run under the law, the "left-hand kingdom of God." The law must and does account for the fallenness of the world. It demands and coerces. It holds persons responsible. It judges. It aims at the better amid a choice of worsts. Responsible policies are trade-offs between what justice demands and what is possible in an intransigent world; irresponsible policies are often those that are mistakenly shaped by the assumption that love can become a direct principle for public ethics.[100]

Although Benne's framework for public theology has Lutheran characteristics and is written partly in critical dialogue with Reformed approaches, it identifies and discusses key issues that any model of public theology must consider. This includes the issue of sin and the distinction between God's salvation and human efforts, Christian ethics and its political relevance and application, as well as Christian virtues in relation to responsible policies, necessary trade-offs and ambiguity in a fallen world. In the following I will in particular highlight Benne's notion of a "core vision" of the church and models for interaction between religion and public life.

FEATURES OF PUBLIC THEOLOGY

This chapter has argued for a public understanding of the Christian faith, explored different approaches to public theology, and delineated several forms and models of it. I have argued that public theology can be distinguished from political theologies and liberation theologies. However, I have also argued that the political, the prophetic, and contextual remains characteristics of public theology. In summary, I will close this chapter by highlighting three key features of public theology.

---

99. Ibid., 94–95.

100. Ibid., 95–96. Others have toned down the differences between the Lutheran and Reformed approaches to such issues. See Bedford-Strohm, "Public Theology and Political Ethics," 284.

Firstly, public theology is concerned with theological contributions in the public sphere. Public theology refers to the exchange of perspectives, interpretations, and viewpoints informed by Christian faith and tradition, but although public theology is a theological undertaking, defending the Christian faith is not its primary concern. Public theology seeks rather to defend and protect the common good, the "welfare of the city." A part of this is to defend the public sphere and freedom of expression. It also implies the task of redefining and recreating the public sphere, and self-critically re-examining its own contributions to the public conversation. Accordingly, public theology is challenged to address the issues that are not brought to the attention of the public sphere and to communicate effectively and meaningfully with its secular, non-religious counterparts as well as those of other faiths or religious outlooks. In short, public theology must engage in conversation with Christians, people of religion and non-religion, the secular, and the marginalized.

Secondly, public theology is a contextual enterprise, being self-critically conscious of how it is embedded in a specific cultural context and reflecting critically on this culture. Public theology needs to consider carefully the contexts to which it speaks as well as the even more difficult reflexive question, how it depends on and is shaped by its very context. This implies that public theology needs to be explicit about its rootedness in a particular setting and its particular perspective. At the same time, public theology needs to be a glocal engagement. Crisis and challenges in all parts of the world are interlinked—if not causally, then politically and certainly morally. Public theology must see itself as a glocal task and needs to address the challenges of a global world and how church and society can respond to these in a critical and constructive fashion. As public theology invites perspectives and contributions from different locations, it needs to speak to all of these. It is in this sense that public theology is not only a task and challenge, but also a gift. Public theology makes Christian thought and ideas accessible to a wider audience, thus enriching and giving direction to the ongoing debates on current issues and social concerns.

Thirdly, public theology is a normative and political undertaking. Public theology not only seeks to contribute constructively to public discourse, but also to political discourses. Public theology is challenged to make normative assessments both of the quality of the public sphere as well as with regard to the substantive issues addressed in public debate. This implies difficult assessments of how, to what extent, and with what kind of specificity the theological voice should be heard and how to find the right balance or approach to realism and utopianism. In this way, public theology seeks to reform the given political institutions that structure and dominate public and political life and, indeed, the everyday lives of ordinary men and women around the world.

These three features are widely shared by both practitioners and scholars of public theology. Still, public theology remains a complex and contested field, understood and practiced in a wide range of different ways. This is, not least, because of the problems to be addressed in this book: the problems of social analysis, politics and ethics, as well as language and voice. The problem of social analysis refers to the relationship between theology and social analysis or social science in the field. Both practitioners and scholars of public theology need to establish how social analysis is integrated in, or added on to, the theological outlook and concerns of public theology. Similarly, the problem of politics of ethics can be approached in different ways. Some find the political role of the church, Christian organizations, or individuals to be quite limited. To the extent that they do act politically, it is in their capacity as being citizens, not as Christians or a Christian community. The problem of language and voice relates to both. How should the social analysis be articulated? What should Christian ethics and political involvement be like? Should it take a revolutionary or a more reformist approach? Should public theology be articulated in the particular religious language of the Christian tradition or in a secular and assumedly more accessible language?

Times of crisis call for both social analysis and immanent action, but this only adds to the difficulty and complexity of public theology. How can churches and Christians analyze social challenges and contribute to public and political discussion? How should theology address suffering, injustice, and other social and political issues without losing its Christian characteristics? Indeed, what should public theology look like in times of crisis? These are questions that will be addressed in the following chapters.

4

Times of Crisis

Times of crisis represent a challenge to public theology in many different ways. Not only is it a challenge to read the signs of the times appropriately, but it is also essential to find ways to respond to this crisis with prudence and integrity. In this chapter I will introduce three examples of public theology in practice. All of them explicitly define themselves as theological responses to a political, social, economic, cultural, and religious crisis and all of them make use of the Greek term *kairos* to interpret this crisis. The three documents to be considered are therefore milestones in what can be called *kairos theology*. Before looking more closely at how these kairos documents deal with the problems of public theology (in chapters 5, 6 and 7), I will in this chapter present their social setting, contents, and characteristics.

THE KAIROS DOCUMENTS

In 1985 church leaders and lay Christians in South Africa issued what came to be known as the *Kairos Document* (hereafter *Kairos South Africa*; KSA).[1] This was a strong denunciation of the apartheid system and its theological legitimation. Only a few years later, and inspired by this South African document, Christians from seven developing countries and three continents issued *The Road to Damascus* (RD).[2] This statement was, in many

---

1. Catholic Institute for International Relations, *Kairos Document*.
2. Catholic Institute for International Relations, *Road to Damascus*.

ways, similar to the South African document, but it addressed international topics and condemned colonialism, imperialism, and capitalism. In both cases a description and interpretation of social processes and events were accompanied by a theological and normative assessment, as well as a moral challenge to act and bring about change. Twenty years later, in December 2009, a group of Palestinian Christians published a document they called *A Moment of Truth: Kairos Palestine* (hereafter only *Kairos Palestine*; KP).[3] Combining insights from Christian theology and social analysis in a manner similar to the other two documents, the authors described what they argued was, and still is, the reality in occupied Palestinian territories.

These are not the only theological or church-related documents that address crisis and combine theological reflection with social analysis and ethics. One other obvious example is the Barmen-declaration given by leading Christians faced with the Nazi-regime in Germany in the early 1930s. Another is *Evangelical Witness*, a response by Concerned Evangelicals to the first kairos document that embraced the key message of *Kairos South Africa*. Several other statements made by Christians, congregations, and churches, be it mainline churches, independent churches, national councils of churches, and international umbrella organizations such as the Lutheran World Federation and the World Council of Churches, could have been examined more closely. However, in this context I choose to focus on kairos documents that represent a vital voice in contemporary theological and political debates, and explicitly see themselves as public and theological responses to crisis situations.

Besides these three, there are several other kairos documents that have been issued in Europe, India, the United States, and elsewhere.[4] All of these documents are, however, informed by the South African kairos document. In this way *Kairos South Africa* plays an important and constitutive role in kairos theology and therefore it deserves special attention. Further, *The Road to Damascus* stands out as an international document and *Kairos Palestine* as the most recent among the kairos documents. This gives reason to include all three of these documents in the following discussion. There are, however, noteworthy differences. Their different contexts and challenges are followed by differences in emphasis, social analysis ,and theological assessments. Yet, all of them are attempts at interpreting, understanding, and critiquing contemporary society and social challenges of their time. They

3. Kairos Palestine, *Moment of Truth*.
4. A number of kairos documents have been compiled in Leonardo, *Kairos Documents*.

Times of Crisis

combine theological reflection and social analysis, and they draw normative conclusions from their inquiry. The desire to change society provides an explicit starting point, and the documents do not avoid explicit normative conclusions that relate to current political issues.

The shared traits of these documents indicate the key features of what can be termed kairos theology: the kind of theology articulated in, and developed through, these (and other related) kairos documents. Accordingly, kairos theology is closely related to the genre of these statements.[5] The documents are neither theological sermons nor are they primarily academic contributions or official church documents. All of them are signed by members of a number of different churches, but they have not been approved by official church bodies and are, in fact, rather presented to churches as a challenge to respond. Yet, they are social, political statements motivated and informed by an ecumenical Christian outlook.

Accordingly, the kairos documents are expressions of theological, ethical reflection, but also of critical, applied social analysis. They denounce false theologies, exploitation, and oppression, and identify ways of promoting justice and peace. In short, they are examples of public theology in times of crisis.

APARTHEID IN SOUTH AFRICA

The South African document presents itself as "a Christian, biblical and theological comment on the political crisis" (KSA, preface to the first edition) in the country, and states:

> The time has come. The moment of truth has arrived. South Africa has been plunged into a crisis that is shaking the foundations and there is every indication that the crisis has only just begun and that it will deepen and become even more threatening in the months to come. It is the KAIROS or moment of truth not only for apartheid but also for the church and all other faiths and religions. (KSA 1)[6]

---

5. Robert McAfee Brown has also pointed out the connection between these types of statements, and used the term kairos theology. However, his analysis does not include *Kairos Palestine*, but the South African, Central American documents, as well as *The Road to Damascus* (Brown, *Kairos*). See also Buttelli, "Public Theology" and Le Bruyns, "The Rebirth of Kairos Theology?".

6. Citations from *Kairos South Africa* are, if not otherwise stated, from the revised, second edition from 1986.

That this is a contextually rooted document is confirmed not only by its contents, but also in the way the writing, editing, and publishing of the document is presented. It has come into being through repeated discussion groups where different drafts have been put under critical analysis. In this sense, the document can be considered a people's document. At the same time, it is evidently informed by scholarly theology. There are references both to the New Testament scholars Cullmann and Käsemann (in footnotes 9 and 10) and the systematic theologian Bonhoeffer (KSA 3.3). Accordingly, *Kairos South Africa* comes across as an example of contextual, popular, and informed public theology. Considering the list of signatories, the document received support from representatives of a wide range of churches and denominations.[7]

Kairos South Africa addresses the situation in South Africa in the mid-1980s. At that time South Africa's apartheid system had been in place for several decades, and had become an integrated part of South African law, politics, and social life. The immediate background for *Kairos South Africa* was the brutality of the apartheid regime and the growing resistance against it. The document refers to escalating confrontations between the authorities with young black men and women, and argues that circumstances are changing. South Africa is in a kairos situation.[8]

The roots to apartheid can be found in the European colonization of South Africa, first Dutch and then British immigration and rule. European immigrants came to constitute the white segment of the population, in contrast to the black indigenous population. Especially in groups of Dutch ancestry, the Boer, the distinction between different races and ethnic groups came to be of fundamental political importance, as many of them supported a segregated society in which different groups had different rights. The apartheid system was a political program geared towards maintaining this segregation. This resulted in separate buses, schools, and swimming pools for the different groups, a ban on mixed marriages, etc.

On June 16 1976 protests by thousands of high school students in the streets of Soweto outside Johannesburg turned into a massacre as the police

---

7. The first version of *Kairos South Africa* (1985) was signed by a number of theologians and church leaders, while the revised version (1986) had so many signatures that these were not included in the second edition.

8. For more on the South African kairos document, see Barkat and Mutmabirwa, *Challenge to the Church*; Logan, *Kairos Covenant*; and Petersen, "Time, Resistance and Reconstruction."

opened fire. The significance of this event can hardly be underestimated. As the South African scholar Robin M. Petersen points out, Soweto signifies:

> a kairotic turning point in our history and in our consciousness of history, an explosive shifting of paradigms, of the arrival of something new, a *novum* that breaks the "bounds of possibility," that opens up new terrain and requires from us new maps, including the theological ones.[9]

In retrospect the events in Soweto stand out as a turning point in the resistance against apartheid. Along with increasing internal resistance came mounting international protest. Opposition was organized partly internally in the country and partly abroad, especially in the rand zone countries of Namibia, Botswana, and Zimbabwe. The African National Congress (ANC) was the main resistance group with Nelson Mandela as an imprisoned, but nevertheless important, front figure of the movement.

The South African kairos document is a Christian and theological expression of this resistance movement. It criticizes various forms of theology that legitimize apartheid, outlines an alternative theology, and challenges the churches and others to resist through practical action. This is done with a combination of a unique conceptual apparatus and more traditional perspectives. The chapter on "state theology" is thus introduced with a discussion of the Christian's relationship to the authorities based on Paul's letter to the Romans (Rom 13:1–7). This is a core text in theological discussion of state-church relations. *Kairos South Africa* also discusses key hermeneutical principles that should be used when such biblical texts are read and emphasizes the need for a critical distance to the text and its current application.

This is followed by a discussion of two key biblical themes: the contrast between chaos and order, and respect for the political authorities as legislator and upholder of social order. These topics are related to the situation in South Africa in the mid-1980s, as the government's understanding of law and order is challenged and given an alternative interpretation. What the authors term *state theology* legitimizes the apartheid policies of the South African government which *Kairos South Africa* sees as an expression of fear of communism and secularism, reflecting the ideological climate of the Cold War. Communism and secularism are considered linked, while the free world involves free religious exercise, national self-determination,

---

9. Petersen, "Theological Reflection on Public Policy," 76, original emphasis.

and prosperity. Accordingly, communism is seen to undermine the state's foundation and the labelling of critics as communists becomes a way of making them enemies of the state. The inadequacy of such accusations is underlined in the kairos document.

While state theology was articulated and defended by the primarily Afrikaans-speaking churches, *church theology* was the dominant theology of the English-speaking churches. The latter is characterized by a desire for reconciliation between the oppressors and the oppressed. The South African document points out, however, that there are key similarities between these two forms of theology. They both have a desire for reconciliation between the parties in the South African conflict. The authors describe this as a reconciliation of right and wrong that neither can nor should be reconciled. It is a kind of reconciliation that maintains the status quo and sustains the social system that state theology legitimizes. In practice, church theology has the same legitimizing function as state theology.

The analysis of justice is similar to the analysis of reconciliation in that it addresses the use and understanding of a central theological idea. Church theology's emphasis and expectation of justice implies, according to the kairos authors, a continuation of the form of injustice that state theology defends. Similarly, church theology's rejection of violence in the face of injustice is criticized for a lack of nuance and a narrow understanding of violence. In short, these forms of theology suffer from fundamental shortcomings: a lack of social analysis.

Accordingly, the kairos authors argue that critical social analysis is necessary to bring about a constructive, prudent, and contextual theology in South Africa. Their constructive contribution is what they call a *prophetic theology* that addresses oppression and suffering and responds critically and constructively to it.[10] They write:

> To be truly prophetic, our response would have to be, in the first place, solidly grounded in the Bible. Our KAIROS impels us to return to the Bible and to search the Word of God for a message that is relevant to what we are experiencing in South Africa today. (…)
>
> Consequently a prophetic response and a prophetic theology would include a reading of the signs of the times. This is what the great Biblical prophets did in their times and this is what Jesus tells us to do. When the Pharisees and Sadducees ask for a sign from

---

10. In the 1986 edition, it is especially the chapter on prophetic theology that has changed (see footnotes in the revised version).

Times of Crisis

heaven, he tells them to "read the signs of the times" (Mt. 16:3) or to "interpret this KAIROS" (Lk. 12:56). (KSA 4.1)

Prophetic theology is therefore perceived as a combination of social analysis and theological reflection. Social analysis is seen as the starting point for the theological work and biblical texts and the Christian tradition are read and interpreted on the basis of this social analysis. Thus social analysis and the classic theological work are drawn closely together in this kind of prophetic theology. The social analysis points to the problems oppression, injustice, and human suffering, but at the same time the classic characteristics of theological work remain of key importance: the Bible and the Christian tradition. In fact, suffering and oppression set the agenda for the interpretation of the biblical texts and the Christian tradition.

OPPRESSION IN THE GLOBAL SOUTH

The document *The Road to Damascus: Kairos and Conversion* was published just a few years after *Kairos South Africa*, in 1989. It was inspired by the South African document, but also by a Central American kairos document: *Kairos Central America: A Challenge to the Churches of the World*. In the introduction, the signatories explain the aim and structure of the document:

> We, the signatories of this document, are Christians from different church traditions in seven different nations: the Philippines, South Korea, Namibia, South Africa, El Salvador, Nicaragua and Guatemala. What we have in common is not only a situation of violent and political conflict, but also the phenomenon of Christians on both sides of the conflict. This is accompanied by the development of a Christian theology that sides with the poor and the oppressed and the development of a Christian theology that sides with the oppressor. This is both a scandal and a crisis that challenges the Christian people of our countries. (. . .)
>
> The purpose of this document is not simply to deplore the divisions among Christians or to exhort both sides to seek unity. We wish to lay bare the historical and political roots of the conflict (Chapter 1), to affirm the faith of the poor and the oppressed Christians in our countries (Chapter 2), to condemn the sins of those who oppress, exploit, persecute and kill people (Chapter 3), and to call to conversion those who have strayed from the truth of

Christian faith and commitment (Chapter 4). The time has come for us to take a stand and to speak out.

The immediate context for *The Road to Damascus* is not as tangible as the events that occasioned *Kairos South Africa*. This is an international document and should be understood in light of the wider global context and more specifically the conditions in the developing world and international political, ideological, and financial trends in the 1980s.

Decolonization, the creation of the United Nations, and international development cooperation after WWII reflected and created great expectations in the global South for economic growth, prosperity, and a better future. Different development theories and strategies succeeded each other, but still the developing world was unable to catch up with the rich industrial countries. World poverty seemed to remain a constant and key economists came to see international trade more as an exploitative and repressive mechanism than a means to new growth. In particular, the Marxist inspired analysis of the dependency school articulated such concerns.[11] In addition, the Cold War conflict between East and West was felt in countries around the world as a political, ideological, and economic battle for influence. In different forms of liberation theologies this was given a theological interpretation.

In *The Road to Damascus* the authors draw up these conflict lines between rich and poor, oppressors and oppressed, and then they examine the causes of this conflict in terms of colonialism and imperialism. This puts the document in the context of North-South conflict and Western imperialism rather than the East-West conflict and the divide of the Cold war. The authors describe "the people's struggle against colonialism" and place themselves on the side of the people in the fight against colonialism, foreign control, and exploitation.

The call for a nuanced social analysis made in *Kairos South Africa* is also heard here. *The Road to Damascus* distinguishes between war and various types of conflict, not least between low-intensity conflict and full war. It is argued that the current situation is one of such low-intensity conflict with costs in the form of suffering and oppression. The authors deplore a situation in which Christians are to be found on both sides of a conflict, but, as in *Kairos South Africa*, a harmonizing reconciliation between the parties of the conflict is rejected.

---

11. Amin, *Accumulation on a World Scale*.

In *The Road to Damascus* too there is a strong emphasis on the faith and theology that is found among the poor. The faith of the poor is confronted with the faith and the images of God that were presented to them by colonial officials. Thus a theological break with the past, colonialism, and imperialism, as well as its theology, is called for. This becomes the starting point for an alternative prophetic theology.

This kind of theology is expounded not, as in *Kairos South Africa*, in relation to state and church theologies, but in contrast to idolatry, secularization, heresy, hypocrisy, and blasphemy. Idolatry is understood as "the sin of worshipping or being subservient to someone or something which is not God" (RD 49) and "right-wing Christianity" (RD 63) in particular is described as heretical. Hypocrisy refers to church leaders who remain silent or "claim to be non-partisan" (RD 78). This is the part that most closely matches the treatment of the church theology in *Kairos South Africa* while the discussion of blasphemy parallels the discussion of state theology in the South African document.

The South African kairos document and *The Road to Damascus* also have in common that they both discuss the crises they are addressing in relation to Empire. In the South African document the State emerges as the Empire, while in *The Road to Damascus* colonialism, imperialism, and economic control (RD 3–5 and 9–12) are expressions of the same. Both documents make a comparison with the first Christians and their relationship to the Roman Empire: "in earlier times when Christians rejected the gods of the Roman Empire they were branded as 'atheists'—by the State" (KSA 2.3) and "[t]he early Christians were considered a threat by the Roman empire" (RD 2).

It is noteworthy how suffering, oppression, and criticism are not the last words in this document. The last chapter is written under the heading "the call to repentance." This call to repentance is associated with the concept of kairos and specifically to Saul's conversion as described in Acts 9:1–19. Repentance is seen as a challenge to "all who in the name of God support the persecution of Christians who side with the poor" (RD 86). Moreover the radical element in this call to repentance is emphasized, not least through an explicit rejection of serving "two masters" (RD 87). Prophetic theology is presented as both a constructive theology and one that explores and suggests concrete actions in response to crisis.

INTERRUPTION AND IMAGINATION

WAR IN PALESTINE

The third document, *A Moment of Truth: Kairos Palestine*, was published in December 2009 and is written by Palestinian theologians and church leaders. Several of them have, or have had, leading positions in the church and Christian organizations. In the preface to the document, they write:

> This document is the Christian Palestinians' word to the world about what is happening in Palestine. It is written at this time when we wanted to see the Glory of the grace of God in this land and in the sufferings of its people. In this spirit the document requests the international community to stand by the Palestinian people who have faced oppression, displacement, suffering and clear apartheid for more than six decades. The suffering continues while the international community silently looks on at the occupying State, Israel. Our word is a cry of hope, with love, prayer and faith in God. We address it first of all to ourselves and then to all the churches and Christians in the world, asking them to stand against injustice and apartheid, urging them to work for a just peace in our region, calling on them to revisit theologies that justify crimes perpetrated against our people and the dispossession of the land. (KP Preface)

In other words, *Kairos Palestine* is a response to the situation in the Middle East and more specifically, the conflict between Israel and Palestine. The authors of the document point to the "security wall" Israel has built between Israel and Palestine, a "cruel war" in 2008–2009, and the "inhuman conditions" in Gaza as the immediate background to the document. Given these circumstances they find that the current situation represents an acute crisis. In the introduction to the document their agony is made even more evident. They write:

> We, a group of Christian Palestinians, after prayer, reflection and an exchange of opinion, cry out from within the suffering in our country, under the Israeli occupation, with a cry of hope in the absence of all hope, a cry full of prayer and faith in a God ever vigilant, in God's divine providence for all the inhabitants of this land. Inspired by the mystery of God's love for all, the mystery of God's divine presence in the history of all peoples and, in a particular way, in the history of our country, we proclaim our word based on our Christian faith and our sense of Palestinian belonging—a word of faith, hope and love. (KP Introduction)

The final words in this paragraph can also be found in the document's subtitle: *A word of faith, hope and love from the heart of Palestinian suffering.* Thus, already at the very beginning, the basic structure and key features of the document's concerns and contents are signaled to the reader. The trinity of faith, hope, and love provides a biblical reference (1 Cor 13) and proclaims the theological character of the document.

The situation in Palestine must be understood in light of the tensions and conflict in the Middle East after World War II and the founding of the state of Israel in 1948. This meant that large groups of Palestinians fled from their homes to neighboring countries and beyond. The following wars indicate the controversies this created. The Arab-Israeli War, when Israel expanded its territory considerably at the expense of the Palestinian territories in 1948–9, was followed by the Suez War between Israel and Egypt in 1956. In 1967 came the Six-Day War, when Israel made a pre-emptive strike against Egypt. In 1973, the October War, or the Yom Kippur War, followed. More recently there have been several periods of war and violence between Israeli and various Palestinian groups. The Palestinian uprising, the First Intifada, in the 1980s and the Second Intifada from 2000 onwards deserve special mention.

The borders between Israel and its neighbors have changed with the wars in the area. The Palestinian autonomous areas consist today of the West Bank and Gaza. Recognition of the autonomy of these areas can be seen as a step towards the creation of a two-state solution to the conflict and the security wall between the countries is a visible expression of a separation between the two. As the conflict and the Israeli settlement policies have continued, a two-state solution seems increasingly unlikely.

Kairos Palestine also emerges out of a specific multi-religious context and the document's invitation to dialogue and cooperation across religious divides represents a new feature of kairos theology. Importantly, however, the critical voice in the document does not address human suffering and the socio-political conditions alone. It also assesses religion and religious actors. As in the other two documents, proponents of alternative interpretations of the Christian faith are criticized and encouraged to change their theology and their interpretation of the scriptures. In fact, *Kairos Palestine* offers a comprehensive explanation of its theological outlook, including a reflection on how the Word of God should be understood and a discussion of the understanding of Israel as the Promised Land. This is clearly informed by Palestinian liberation theology as developed by writers such as Naim Ateek,[12] Mitri Raheb,[13] and Munib Younan.[14]

In this document too the authors develop a theology that is closely integrated with the political, social, and ethical analysis in the document. Thus, the religious identity and theological outlook of the authors is both an explicit and an implicit part of the social analysis offered in the document, and this combination of applied theology and social analysis has practical, moral implications. The authors articulate a normative perspective on the current socio-political situation and suggest concrete steps for improving the living conditions in Palestine. In other words, it is not easy to determine when theology begins and social analysis takes over, or vice versa.

Finally, it is worth noting how *Kairos Palestine* addresses multiple recipients or publics: churches, religious leaders, Christians and Muslims, and politicians at home and abroad. There is a strong emphasis on constructive dialogue, especially between Palestinians and Israelis. This dialogue is described as a process between different groups of people, though not as a means of compromise between different theological positions.

To sum up, the religious, political, and moral dimensions, local and international perspectives, and combination of particular concerns and universal outlook gives *Kairos Palestine* a well-considered and complex character. This makes it a strong and powerful statement that questions, challenges, and inspires international cooperation to end the Israeli occupation and human suffering in Palestine.[15]

CRISIS AS KAIROS

In contrast to other kinds of contextual theologies the kairos documents address a specific time or situation and analyze what they see as a profound social, economic, political, and theological crisis. The South African authors find that "South Africa has been plunged into a crisis that is shaking the foundations" (KSA 1) and that this crisis is intensifying. This situation is described as "oppression and tyranny" (KSA 4.1) and as "conflict, crisis

---

12. Ateek, *Justice, and Only Justice* and Ateek, *Palestinian Christian*.
13. Raheb, *I Am a Palestinian Christian*.
14. Younan, *Witnessing for Peace*.
15. For more on *Kairos Palestine*, see Fretheim, "The Power of Invitation"; Le Roux, "Kairos, Palestine"; Katanacho, "Theological Contribution"; and Schmid, "From the Church of the Nativity."

and struggle" (KSA 4.1). In *The Road to Damascus* an important concern is to emphasize the brutality of the current situation and "the everyday reality of human sacrifice" (RD 58). Similarly, *Kairos Palestine* is a response to "Israeli occupation of Palestinian territories, deprivation of our freedom and all that results from this situation" (KP 1.1). The authors see themselves at a "dead end in the tragedy of the Palestinian people" (KP Introduction).

All of these documents use the term *kairos* to describe the context and situation they find themselves in.[16] Often kairos is explained by a comparison with the word *chronos*. Both are Greek words for time, and chronos refers to time that passes through the past, present, and future, as in the word chronological. This notion of linear time is reflected in the biblical narrative. The opening words of the Bible place the creation at the beginning of time and the closing chapters describe a new heaven and a new earth.

The concept of kairos on the other hand denotes the character of a specific moment in time—a "rupture of ordered time"[17]—and with special characteristics, and in the Christian tradition the concept of kairos is in particular linked to Jesus' coming, death, and resurrection.[18] The coming of Jesus Christ implies a qualitative breakthrough and a turning point in history. *Kairos South Africa* cites Luke 19:44: "and all because you did not recognize your opportunity (KAIROS) when God offered it" (KSA 1). With Jesus' resurrection, this turning point receives lasting importance: Jesus brought the Kingdom of God close (Mark 1:15). Thus, in Christian theology kairos often refers to the special quality of a given time and its challenge on God's people to respond appropriately.

In other words, kairos is the moment of revelation—the time when the will of God and the truth are made visible and evident in a special way. This also implies that it comes with special claims and challenges. The

---

16. *Kairos* is one of three Greek words that all relate to crisis although in different ways: *eschaton*, *krisis*, and *kairos*. While *eschaton* refers primarily to the coming future, *krisis* refers to a dangerous or difficult situation with a potential undesirable, negative outcome. Of these three, kairos is the one that most explicitly denotes the time of critical change (Sipiora and Baumlin, *Rhetoric and Kairos*).

17. Chopp, *The Power to Speak*, 48.

18. Although this contrast between *kairos* and *chronos* is often emphasised, the terms are closely related. As Petersen points out, *kairos* is part of *chronos*: ". . . all invocations of *kairos* within prophetic theology (and in particular within the *Kairos Document*), have concentrated on *kairotic* time as historical time, as a particular socio-political conjuncture that is especially significant and that demands decisive action. Hence, although contrasted with *chronos*, it is still a form of chronological time, of history as diachrony" (Petersen, "Time, Resistance and Reconstruction," 13, original emphasis).

kairos moment is a time to convert and change. Accordingly, in Christian theology it is not only necessary to understand what the coming and resurrection of Christ implied in the past, but also to interpret the present (Luke 12:56). It is part of theological inquiry to understand what Jesus' coming and resurrection means today and what the coming of the Kingdom of God to our world means for our understanding of this world, our own time, and our own society.

Consequently, when the kairos authors choose the term kairos to denote the crisis, this reflects an interpretation of the crisis which is not only a social analysis, but also a theological interpretation. The authors of the South African document write that they "see the present crisis or KAIROS as indeed a divine visitation" (KSA conclusion) and a "moment of grace opportunity, the favorable time in which God issues a challenge to decisive action" (KSA 1). *The Road to Damascus* similarly stresses the present kairos is "a time of grace, a God-given opportunity for conversion and hope" (RD 43). Kairos is a time "to take a stand and to speak out" (RD Preamble). Put differently, kairos theology is "the act of interpreting a particular crisis as a kairos in the biblical sense of an encounter with God, who is speaking to us now with warnings, promises and a call to action."[19] In the field of rhetoric, kairos similarly refers to the right moment to act or to speak and this is what the kairos authors have done when issuing these documents.

The challenge to convert is also articulated in all three kairos documents. They speak of "a decisive turnabout on the part of those groups and individuals who have consciously or unconsciously compromised their Christian faith for political, economic and selfish reasons" (RD Preamble), and "a time of repentance for our silence, indifference, lack of communion" (KP 5.2). It is illuminating to understand this kind of repentance in contrast to forms of conversion that are rejected. The South African kairos document distances itself from the "reliance upon 'individual conversions' in response to 'moralising demands' to change the structures of a society" (KSA 3.2). It is not personal, individual sins which matter in the kairos documents, but structural sin that requires structural conversion.

KAIROS AND PUBLIC THEOLOGY

The documents presented in this chapter show how faith and theological resources can not only motivate political engagement by faith-based actors,

19. Nolan, "Kairos Theology," 216.

religious leaders, and Christians, but also how they can inform the way they are publicly and politically involved in the public sphere. Being public statements that engage in a political discourse and articulating a vision of faith, hope, and a different future make them powerful both religiously and politically. The combination of social analysis, theological reflection, and moral commitment as integral parts of one and the same statement, has the same effect. And it is through this merging of fields, ideas, and different discourses that the document informs our understanding of public theology. The kairos documents thus come across not only as multi-dimensional documents, but also as well-considered, clear, and normative statements.

Thus, kairos theology refers to a branch of theology that has made *kairos* a key term in its theological thinking. It is articulated and developed in times of crisis. The term emphasizes how this is no ordinary time, but a special time that are both an opportunity to change and to take action. Kairos theology is ecumenical, contextual, and international theology and social analysis. It is a socially aware, concerned, and committed theology.[20]

With these characteristics the kairos documents and kairos theology invite us to revisit the problems of public theology, and this is the task at hand for the following chapters. They raise complex questions regarding religion and politics, faith and social issues, and not least about Christian theology and social analysis. Taking the most recent kairos document as an example, *Kairos Palestine* invites us to ask not only: What is going on in Palestine?, but also: How should we do public theology? How can we live responsibly and act morally in this time of crisis?

In the following chapters I will examine how the three problems of public theology are dealt with in kairos theology: the problems of social analysis (chapter 5); politics and ethics (chapter 6); and language and voice (chapter 7).

---

20. Accordingly, as I use the terms *kairos* and *kairos theology* here, it is closely related to the kairos documents. However, kairos theology is not without historical precedence. It both resembles and echoes considerations that led the German-American philosopher and theologian Paul Tillich to make the concept of kairos a central idea in his theology. To him Nazism was a kairos in world history and he argued this ideology represented a crucial point in time that required a critical and active response (Tillich, *Protestant Era*, 32–51 and Tillich, *Systematic Theology*, 393–96). Similarly, Jürgen Moltmann makes use of the concept of kairos in his Christology and eschatology, see Moltmann, *Way of Jesus Christ*; Moltmann, *Coming of God*; and Moltmann, *Ethics of Hope*.

5

Social Analysis

In times of crisis, public theology needs to have an understanding of the social, political, economic, and cultural issues at stake. In short, public theology needs a social analysis. But what can, and should, public theology say about social issues in times of crisis?

This chapter will address this problem of social analysis in public theology by first discussing how social analysis features in kairos theology and then looking at the implicit understanding of the relationship between theology and the social sciences. Contrary to the notion that the two represent distinct and contrary disciplines and approaches, I suggest viewing theology and social sciences as overlapping disciplines with considerable points of contact. I argue that public theology implies that they need to be combined and that perspectives and insights from both need to be integrated into the field.

EXTRAORDINARY REALITY

As shown in the previous chapter, the authors of the kairos documents find that they live in extraordinary times and a crisis marked by profound and acute challenges. This reflects how they rely on an analysis of the social conditions of their time and contexts, but also provides the context for their call for a new understanding of society and current social issues.

In the South African document this is put forward as a need to replace what they call church theology. The authors write:

> We have seen how 'Church Theology' tends to make use of absolute principles like reconciliation, negotiation, non-violence and peaceful solutions and applies them indiscriminately and uncritically to all situations. Very little attempt is made to analyze what is actually happening in our society and why it is happening. It is not possible to make valid moral judgements about a society without first understanding that society. The analysis of apartheid that underpins 'Church Theology' is simply inadequate. The present crisis has now made it very clear that the efforts of church leaders to promote effective and practical ways of changing our society have failed. This failure is due in no small measure to the fact that 'Church theology' has not developed a social analysis that would enable it to understand the mechanics of injustice and oppression. (KSA 3.4)

Accordingly, to these kairos authors the fundamental problem of church theology is a lack of social analysis. The authors argue that theology needs a social analysis which is context sensitive and which moves beyond "absolute principles" and abstract descriptions of the situation. Only then can it "make valid judgements" of "what is actually happening."

This call for social analysis is articulated also in the other two kairos documents. In its effort to understand "what is actually happening [and] why it is happening," the social analysis in *The Road to Damascus* focuses on the effects of historical colonialization and contemporary imperialism:

> The effects of imperialism upon the Third World form a litany of woes: our children die of malnutrition and disease, there are no jobs for those who want to work, families break up to pursue employment abroad, peasants and indigenous communities are displaced from their land, most urban dwellers have to live in unsanitary slums, many women have to sell their bodies, too many die without having lived a life that human persons deserve. We also suffer because of the plunder of our natural resources, and then we ourselves are being blamed for it. (RD 12)

Here *The Road to Damascus* makes a causal connections between international imperialism and domestic and local social conditions, but their primary concern is to unfold the current living conditions for children, the unemployed, urban dwellers etc. The emphasis is on the social realities of the time. In this sense, the analysis is empirical and inductive rather than deductive from the premise of imperialist exploitation.

INTERRUPTION AND IMAGINATION

In *Kairos Palestine* it is the immediate and contemporary context of Israeli settlement policies and the occupation of Palestinian territories that is the starting point and primary focus of the social analysis. Here too it is the social and political consequences that are highlighted:

> Israeli settlements ravage our land in the name of God and in the name of force, controlling our natural resources, including water and agricultural land, thus depriving hundreds of thousands of Palestinians, and constituting an obstacle to any political solution.
>
> Reality is the daily humiliation to which we are subjected at the military checkpoints, as we make our way to jobs, schools or hospitals.
>
> Reality is the separation between members of the same family, making family life impossible for thousands of Palestinians, especially where one of the spouses does not have an Israeli identity card. (KP 1.1.2, 1.1.3 and 1.1.4)

The use of the term "reality" in these paragraphs indicates a focus on speaking about the social and political conditions at hand in a straight forward manner. This parallels the other documents' focus on "what is actually happening."

The kairos authors thus seem concerned to give a truthful witness about the "reality on the ground" and, in particular in *Kairos Palestine*, the notion of truth is used to identify legitimate and relevant interpretations and descriptions of the situation. As there are true versions of what is going on and false ones, truth functions as an analytical criterion. Truth corresponds with realities on the ground. False versions of what is happening simply do not match these realities. Accordingly, the social analysis is presented as a representation of reality as this reality actually is, and they contrast their interpretations with others' interpretations that are consequently dismissed. One illustrative example is how the authors write that while "everyone is speaking about peace in the Middle East (. . .) the reality is one of Israeli occupation of Palestinian territories, deprivation of our freedom and all that results from this situation" (KP 1.1). This also gives context to their explicit warning against "a reversal of reality":

> In the face of this reality, Israel justifies its actions as self-defence, including occupation, collective punishment and all other forms of reprisals against the Palestinians. In our opinion, this vision is a reversal of reality. Yes, there is Palestinian resistance to the occupation. However, if there were no occupation, there would be no resistance, no fear and no insecurity. This is our understanding of

the situation. Therefore, we call on the Israelis to end the occupation. Then they will see a new world in which there is no fear, no threat but rather security, justice and peace. (KP 1.4)

Later in *Kairos Palestine* there is a similar talk of twisting the truth: The authors "call on Israel to give up its injustice towards us, not to twist the truth of reality of the occupation by pretending that it is a battle against terrorism. The roots of "terrorism" are in the human injustice committed and in the evil of the occupation" (KP 4.3). Here too the distinction between true and false is considered (relatively) clear cut, and the truth is regarded as twisted if it does not match the interpretation and description of the kairos authors.

In fact, the Israeli occupation is the key reference point for what is said in *Kairos Palestine* about "the reality" and the situation in Palestine. This is described in detail in terms such as plundering, humiliation, bondage, and discrimination, and includes reference to a wide range of specific political issues and controversies: the Israeli "separation wall" (KP 1.1.1), Israeli settlements (KP 1.1.2), military checkpoints (KP 1.1.3), refugees (1.1.6), prisoners (KP 1.1.7), Jerusalem (KP 1.1.8), discriminatory policies (KP 1.2.1), emigration (KP 1.3), collective punishment (KP 1.4) etc. In this way, also *Kairos Palestine* puts a strong focus on the effects that current policies, power structures, and conflict have on ordinary people's everyday life.

CONFLICT AND STATUS QUO

This identification of conflict and power is a core element in the kairos documents' social analysis. The inequality, injustice, and suffering are seen as a result of structural conflicts in society. In the South African document the relationship between white and black in South Africa under apartheid is seen as a conflict between the "oppressor and the oppressed" (KSA 1) and in light of the wider context of communism and terrorism. Thus *Kairos South Africa* presents us with an ideological interpretation and ideational outlook on the social processes at play.

The social analysis in *The Road to Damascus* has similar traits. In this case though, it is not the policies of a national government that are addressed, but rather the consequences of international or global political structures. Compared to the South African document, there is also a stronger emphasis on economic factors. More specifically it is the international financial regime that is criticized and, accordingly, the macro-political dimension of the social analysis is here coupled with a stronger materialistic and realistic perspective. The understanding of the relationship between the North and the South echoes Marxist inspired dependency theories, and ties social realities in the global South countries closely with living conditions in the North.

The conflicts identified by the kairos documents also tend to be seen as irreconcilable and are frequently referred to by using the term *war*. The South African authors argue they are facing a conflict "in which one side is right and the other wrong" (KSA 3.1) and that the situation in South Africa is one of "civil war or revolution" (KSA 4.1, first edition). *The Road to Damascus* speaks of "the total war being waged against the people, leading to the death and destruction of our communities" (RD 47). This document also makes a distinction between low-intensity conflict and full war, and describes the current situation in the so-called Third World as a "dirty war" (RD 77). Similarly, the Palestinian document highlights the "duty to liberate [this land] from the evil of injustice and war" (KP 2.3.1; see also 2.5 and 3.5).

The overall goal of all these documents is thus to address the status quo and its implicit conflicts. They also argue that to support the status quo is to maintain these conflicts. The South African authors write: "The State makes use of the concept of law and order to maintain the status quo which it depicts as 'normal'. But this *law* is the unjust and discriminatory laws of apartheid and this *order* is the organized and institutionalized disorder of oppression" (KSA 2.2, original emphasis). What is described as normal is therefore not the same as the desirable. Similarly, *The Road to Damascus* warns against "a *conscious* defence of the status quo" (RD 45, original emphasis).

Against this background, a key concern for the kairos authors is to create a space for social criticism that addresses the conflict, but is not defined by it. This is illustrated for example in *Kairos South Africa* by how the authors seek to avoid being labelled as communists. They deplore that "[a]nything that threatens the status quo is labelled 'communist'" (KSA 2.3), and that "the state uses the label 'communist' in an uncritical and unexamined way as its symbol of evil" (KSA 2.3). Similarly, *The Road to Damascus* argues that "all real change [is presented] as communist and therefore atheist" (RD 60) and that while the government is presented as democratic, those who work for change are discredited as communists (RD 21). They also find the same mechanism among theological opponents, in particular among representatives of right-wing Christianity. They regard this kind of Christianity as "fanatically *anti-communist*" (RD 71, original emphasis). In the Palestinian document the image of the enemy is another, but the perspective and analysis much the same. In the context of Israeli occupation and the war on terror, the authors insist that social criticism must be possible without being "caricatured as terrorists" (KP 5.4.1). They reject being defined as "enemies only because we declare that we want to live as free people in our land" (KP 2.3.4).[1]

NEUTRALITY, COMPROMISE, AND CHOICE

In line with the strong focus on irreconcilable conflict in their social analysis, another key feature in these kairos documents is the rejection of neutrality and compromise. This is expressed for example in how the South African document outlines two responses to the kairos moment it is addressing. One is passive and rejected: "We cannot just sit back and wait for the oppressor to see the light so that the oppressed can put out their hands and beg for the crumbs of some small reforms. That in itself would be degrading and oppressive" (KSA 3.2). The criticism of the church theology relates in particular to the understanding that it makes "a virtue of neutrality and sitting on the sidelines" (KSA 3.4). In contrast, the authors argue: "The attempt to remain neutral in this kind of conflict is futile. Neutrality enables the status quo of oppression (and therefore violence) to continue. It is a way of giving tacit support to the oppressor, a support for brutal violence" (KSA 3.3).

In *The Road to Damascus* there is a similar sharp critique of any attempt to be neutral. The authors make it clear that there is no neutral middle position where one can, with integrity, position oneself outside of the conflict. This is addressed as an issue of hypocrisy and resembles the analysis of church theology in *Kairos South Africa*. Hypocrisy is explained with reference to the "hypocrisy of the scribes and Pharisees" (RD 76) and regarded as particularly evident when "those who claim to be non-partisan and talk of keeping the balance (. . .) betray their partisanship by criticizing

---

1. A related terminology is used in the dichotomy of security vs. insecurity. *The Road to Damascus* finds that a conflict is constructed between "their security [and] our insecurity" (RD 53) and deplores that "the Church and its theology is seen as a dangerous threat to the national security state" (RD 73). Similarly, the Palestinian authors find that "the freedom of access to the holy places is denied under the pretext of security" (KP 1.1.5).

mainly those who question the status quo" (RD 78). Similarly, silence is rejected as "worse than hypocrisy—a mask for their complicity" (RD 77).

In *Kairos Palestine* the authors criticize decision makers' inability or unwillingness to address and deal with "the tragedy of the Palestinian people." The crisis in the Middle East is explained by how: "decision-makers content themselves with managing the crisis rather than committing themselves to the serious task of finding a way to resolve it" (KP Introduction). The authors point not only to "Israeli disregard of international law and international resolutions," but also to "the paralysis of the Arab world and the international community in the face of this contempt" (KP 1.2). This lack of action makes the international community responsible for the Palestinian suffering. The international community is thus explicitly targeted not as an outsider to, but an integral part of, the problems Palestinians face and the solution to them.

The social analysis in these documents is thus not only a description of the present state and a rejection of compromise, but also a challenge to choose sides. Consequently, the other response outlined in kairos theology is to take a stand, to confront, resist, and struggle. The South African authors describe this as a prophetic stand and state:

> Our present kairos calls for a response from Christians that is biblical, spiritual, pastoral and, above all, prophetic. It is not enough in these circumstances to repeat generalized Christian principles. We need a bold and incisive response that does not give the impression of sitting on the fence but is clearly and unambiguously taking a stand. (KSA 4, first edition)

Kairos South Africa also claims that "Prophetic theology (. . .) faces us with this fundamental choice that admits of no compromises" (KSA 4.3). Similarly, *The Road to Damascus* argues one must choose either compromise or the position of the "progressive Christians" (RD 78). Thus, both documents outline alternative forms of theology: state theology and church theology vs. prophetic theology in *Kairos South Africa*, and right-wing theology vs. progressive, liberation theology in *The Road to Damascus*. In both cases there is only one acceptable alternative and it cannot be combined with a compromise with the others.

It is noteworthy how this kind of social analysis leads to an analysis of not only the social realities, but also contemporary churches and theologies. In fact, a recurrent feature of the documents is that churches are described with much of the same features as the social situation in general.

Social Analysis

The South African authors write: "Both oppressor and oppressed claim loyalty to the same Church. They are both baptized in the same baptism and participate together in the breaking of the same bread, the same body and blood of Christ" (KSA 1). This does not, however, prevent the authors from pointing out the conflict: "*the Church is divided*" (KSA 1, original emphasis), and that "[e]ven within the same denomination there are in fact two Churches" (KSA 1). *Kairos South Africa* writes: "We are a divided Church precisely because not all the members of our Churches have taken sides against oppression" and united themselves with God "who is always on the side of the oppressed" (Ps 103:6; KSA 5.1). Also *The Road to Damascus* describes a "conflict between Christians in the world" (RD Conclusion) and argues that the churches themselves have become a "*site of struggle*" (RD 27, original emphasis). Similarly, the Palestinian kairos authors lament the division of the church and ask sister churches "not to offer a theological cover-up for the injustice we suffer, for the sin of the occupation imposed upon us" (KP 6.1).

TRUTH AND THEOLOGY

This focus on church division and theological disputes indicates how the emphasis on social analysis does not imply that the authors have side-lined their Christian faith or theological insights when doing their social analysis. Indeed, they analyze the social situation in a faith perspective and give the social conditions a theological interpretation. As it is put in *The Road to Damascus*: "As Christians, we look at our situation with eyes that have read the Bible stories" (RD 1). Similarly the South African document argues: "[i]t is in the light of the Biblical teaching about suffering, oppression and tyranny that our prophetic theology must begin to analyze our KAIROS and read the signs of the time" (KS 4.3).

As already noted, the South African document deals in particular with two kinds of theologies that the authors criticize: state theology and church theology. What they describe as state theology refers to "the theological justification of the status quo with its racism, capitalism and totalitarianism. It blesses injustice, canonizes the will of the powerful and reduces the poor to passivity, obedience and apathy" (KSA 2). As it misuses "theological concepts and biblical texts for its own political purposes" (KSA 2), this is rejected. They consider it "heretical theology" (KSA 2.3) and "blasphemous"

INTERRUPTION AND IMAGINATION

(KSA 2.4). Similarly, church theology is rejected as its criticism of apartheid is considered "superficial and counter-productive" (KSA 3). Further, the emergence of such theologies is explained with a reference to "*the type of faith and spirituality* that has dominated Church life for centuries" (KSA 3.4, original emphasis). It is argued that this is a kind of spirituality that:

> ... tended to be an other-worldly affair that has very little, if anything at all, to do with the affairs of this world. Social and political matters were seen as worldly affairs that have nothing to do with the spiritual concerns of the Church. Moreover, spirituality has been understood to be purely private and individualistic (KSA 3.4)

It is worth noting where they find their source of this critique: in the Bible. They write "this kind of faith and this type of spirituality has no biblical foundation. The Bible does not separate the human person from the world in which he or she lives; it does not separate the individual from the social or one's private life from one's public life" (KSA 3.4).

This theological criticism concerns not only social analysis and interpretation of the Bible, but also the very understanding of God. In the South African document the authors criticize the image of "a god who exalts the proud and humbles the poor—the very opposite of the God of the Bible" (KSA 2.4). Similarly, in *The Road to Damascus* the authors criticize the God that missionaries and others presented to people in the developing world: "All that was offered to us by this God was an interior and other-worldly liberation. It was a God who dwelt in heaven and in the Temple but not in the world" (RD 30).

The Road to Damascus deals with "right-wing Christianity" (RD 63–71) and refers to those who persecute the Church (RD 73) or come with "vicious attacks on liberation theology" (RD 75).[2] With reference to the South African kairos document that declares apartheid as heretical, the authors boldly "denounce all forms of right-wing Christianity as heretical" (RD 63) as it implies the "conscious or unconscious legitimation of idolatry" (RD 64). With heresy they mean "a form of belief that selects some parts of the Christian message and reject other parts" (RD 62) and they find that:

> Right-wing Christianity (...) distorts even the authority of the Bible by treating it as a book from heaven that must be obeyed without understanding or critical comprehension. In some

---

2. The Santa Fe documents I and II are mentioned explicitly (RD 21, 25 and 75).

countries, this is called fundamentalism. The attempt to find security in blind obedience, absolute certainties and submission to authoritarianism is not faith. It is slavery. "For freedom Christ has set us free; stand fast therefore, and do not submit again to the yoke of slavery" *(Gal 5:1)*. (RD 67)

The authors of *The Road to Damascus* find that this form of theology is determined by "antagonistic *dualisms* (. . .) between the body and the soul, the material and the spiritual" (RD 68, original emphasis). This is deemed to be "against Christian teaching since the Bible reveals only one God creator of the material and the spiritual, the individual and the social" (RD 68) and they criticize what they call "an other-worldly interpretation of the Bible" (RD 70). In this context also the concept of apostasy is mentioned and explained as an extreme version of heresy, namely one that "abandons the Christian faith altogether" (RD 72).

In *Kairos Palestine* too this kind of theological assessment can be found. Here it is not a specific kind of theology, but primarily an analysis of how theology functions in relation to the occupation that is given attention. In a manner similar to the other kairos documents, the authors explicitly denounce theologies that fundamentally contradict their own position. Theologians who use biblical texts to produce such human rights violations are encouraged to "rectify their interpretation" (KP 2.3.3) and the authors declare that the occupation is "a sin against God and humanity because it deprives the Palestinians of their basic human rights, bestowed by God" (KP 2.5). Consequently, they also "declare that any theology, seemingly based on the Bible or on faith or on history, that legitimizes the occupation, is far from Christian teachings" (KP 2.5). In other words, *Kairos Palestine* criticizes groups that they believe contribute to their suffering and oppression: "fundamentalist Biblical interpretation" (KP 2.2.2), "theological cover-up for the injustice we suffer" (KP 6.1), racism, anti-Semitism, Islamophobia, etc. (KP 6.3). They also argue: "religion cannot favor or support any unjust political regime, but must rather promote justice, truth and human dignity" (KP 3.4.3).

It would, however, be wrong to say that various theologies are assessed only by moral criteria or that theology is reduced to political rhetoric. The theological criticism expressed, as well as the theology presented, comes across as deeply rooted in a commitment to fundamental concerns in Christian theology: faith in God and the Word of God. In their discussion of theologies they denounce, the Palestinian authors write:

> And as Christian Palestinians we suffer from the wrong interpretation of some theologians. Faced with this, our task is to safeguard the Word of God as a source of life and not of death, so that "the good news" remains what it is, "good news" for us and for all. In the face of those who use the Bible to threaten our existence as Christian and Muslim Palestinians, we renew our faith in God because we know that the Word of God can not be the source of our destruction. (KP 2.3.4)

These authors explicitly reject a reductionist approach to religion and the Christian faith and:

> ... declare that any use of the Bible to legitimize or support political options and positions that are based upon injustice, imposed by one person on another, or by one people on another, transform religion into human ideology and strip the Word of God of its holiness, its universality and truth (KP 2.4)

This emphasis on "human ideology" seems to indicate a distinction between religion as something of God, while ideology is something human. Accordingly, the authors seem to insist on an understanding of religion as something transcendental, beyond, and above human reflection and political ideologies.

In other words, there is a profound commitment to religious texts and a Christian interpretation of these in kairos theology. Certain interpretations of the religious texts are, however, seen as illegitimate interpretations, both theologically and politically, and a key hermeneutical criterion is their political and moral implications: the extent to which such interpretations represent an infringement of rights and results in violence or injustice. The notions of human rights and justice are used as hermeneutical tools in the authors' reading of religious texts and interpretation of the Christian tradition, but this moral commitment is closely linked to, and an integral part of, this theological-normative outlook. Consequently, kairos theology offers a positioned social analysis where the authors side with the victims of these conflicts and are committed to truth, justice, and dignity.

THEOLOGY AND THE SOCIAL SCIENCES

To summarize, kairos theology offers a conflict oriented social analysis combined with a normative assessment that sees in this conflict a battle and choice between good and bad, right and wrong. In this sense, it is a simplified and not a nuanced and detailed social analysis that is offered. Some degree of simplification is, of course, unavoidable and it would be too much to ask that a presentation of "the reality" covers all its aspects, nuances, paradoxes, and processes in its entirety. Any analysis or description of the social world involves a simplification of a complex world. On the other hand, a simple, one-dimensional dichotomy between true and false, black, or white might run the risk of over-simplification.

Another problem with the social analysis the kairos documents offer is that it seems to imply a naive understanding of the relationship between the social world and its representations. This is the pitfall of positivism, where one optimistically, and with an overdose of confidence, declares that the analytical conclusions match the empirical facts on the ground, as if these were self-evident and not in need of interpretation. At the same time, it is noteworthy that all of the kairos documents stress that their description, interpretation, and analysis both can and should be challenged. The authors say "[t]his is our understanding of the situation" (KP 1.4) and are open for it to be criticized.

Further, the positioned analysis and the primacy given to the experience of the poor and marginalized seem to trump other considerations. This way of understanding and explaining the social reality resembles key features of liberation theology, and commenting on Juan Luis Segundo's *Liberation of Theology*[3] Gregory Baum finds that for Segundo "the hermeneutical circle begins with a new experience that shatters the theologian's inherited world view, connects the ills of society with a hidden cause, and makes him/her see society and culture from a new angle."[4] The problem with this, Baum argues, is that this "initial shattering experience seems to demand no critical examination at all."[5] Consequently, Baum finds it is necessary to "add a new, critical dimension to Segundo's hermeneutical circle. (. . .) Dialogue with other critical thinkers remains a methodological necessity."[6] Similarly, it seems the experience of the poor should not exclude other critical perspectives from the social analysis of public theology.

These problems indicate how the social analysis of kairos theology raises the more general issue of the relationship between theology and the social sciences. And although, kairos theology combine the two, they

---

3. Segundo, *Liberation of Theology*.
4. Baum, "Theological Method," 120.
5. Ibid., 122.
6. Ibid., 123.

have often been considered as irreconcilable as the rights and wrongs the kairos documents describe. Indeed, as the modern social sciences became established as academic disciplines in the nineteenth century, a split between theology and the social sciences soon developed. This relates closely to ideals of the Enlightenment: liberation from traditional and religious authorities and a strong emphasis and trust in human reason and the individual, autonomous subject. Accordingly, the social sciences and modern social theory developed as distinct from theology, seeking to explain social phenomena and modern society with reference to individuals' actions and social processes, rather than invoking the notion of God or referring to any transcendental factors in the analysis. This disenchantment of the world[7] is largely the paradigm in social science even today, making "methodological atheism"[8] the dominant approach.

The founding fathers of modern social science, Max Weber, Karl Marx, and Émile Durkheim, all contributed to this development, but also to a deepened understanding of the basic issues of modern society: emerging capitalism, division of labor, social cohesion etc. More recently Michel Foucault has shown how power is omnipresent,[9] Zygmunt Bauman has pointed out the late modern society's liquid character,[10] Richard Sennett described the tyrannies of intimacy,[11] and Ulrich Beck has given an account of the risk society.[12] These are all examples of comprehensive social analyses and show how this kind of analysis remains an important topic in the social sciences.

As the social sciences have now expanded into a wide range of disciplines and sub-disciplines, however, this comprehensive interpretation of contemporary society has been supplemented by other more limited analyses and today the term "the social sciences" refers to a set of academic disciplines: Sociology, political science, anthropology, political geography, psychology, etc. These disciplines are characterized by different theoretical perspectives and methodological preferences. Important distinctions are made between individual and collective explanations and between methodological individualism and collectivism. While social theory in general is

7. Weber, *The Sociology of Religion*.
8. Berger, *Sacred Canopy*.
9. Foucault, *Discipline and Punish*.
10. Bauman, *Liquid Modernity*.
11. Sennett, *Fall of Public Man*.
12. Beck, *Risk Society*.

Social Analysis

concerned about the relationship between the actor (individual) and structure (society), and the interaction between these, psychology for example emphasizes the individual and sociology the communal aspects of social life.

The social sciences share, however, an empirical orientation and their analyses have an empirical foundation. Theory needs to be tested empirically, and any hypotheses about social life must be open to testing against the empirical findings. Relying on either quantitative or qualitative methodologies this empirical work is characterized by interpretation. This is not to deny the existence of an objective reality, but a reminder that the facts and figures scholars analyze do not make sense on their own. They must be interpreted and interpretation involves placing the empirical findings in a larger context. For this reason, reflexivity is an important element in any social scientific study: the researcher must make an effort to clarify the context and conditions for her analysis and interpretation.

Further, the social sciences are characterized as being critical and normative, and even "liberation sociology" has been suggested.[13] The Enlightenment placed great trust in the ability of human beings to improve their ways individually and in society to improve conditions collectively. Indeed, an important part of the social sciences that emerged in the nineteenth century was their contribution to analyzing society, detecting problems, and suggesting ways of improving society in the future.

Even today, an important element of social research is to identify the problems of social life and to propose measures to deal with social problems. This critical attitude is implicit in what has already been said about empirical data and interpretation. However, the critical attitude is also reflected in the choice of research topic and in the form of conclusions the social scientists draws from her research. Social scientists have a tradition of working especially with the issues related to problems in the community: drug abuse, health policy, prostitution, etc. Thus, a degree of normativity can also be expected in the conclusions and recommendations that follow social research.

This is also evident in the way social scientists argue. One can distinguish between descriptive and normative arguments. With the disciplines empirical foundation, it is clear that the descriptive argument is central in a social research report. Here the ambition is to describe and analyze the facts of social life. Often, however, the argument from the empirical and

---

13. Feagin and Vera, *Liberation Sociology*.

descriptive moves towards the more prescriptive, in the form of criticism of the actual conditions and/or recommendations on possible measures to remedy social problems, better living conditions etc. A good normative recommendation must be based on an well-informed description and analysis of the present conditions, as well as an assessment of what kind of impact the recommendations have in a particular situation.

Turning to theology, this field has primarily been understood in relation to philosophy and religious studies. While philosophy is understood as part of the humanities, theology is rooted in a particular religious tradition and committed to the Christian church and faith. In one sense Christian theology begins with the presupposition that God come to Earth and man in person: his son Jesus Christ. This makes theology focus on the testimony of Jesus and the interpretation of Old and New Testament handed down through the Christian tradition. The claim that religious studies represents a comparative study of religion(s) with a descriptive-oriented outside-perspective, while theology is a normative discipline that studies the Christian faith with an insider's perspective, is, however, misleading. The outsider's perspective is no stranger to theology, although it is often combined with an insider's perspective and a normative ambition.

Just like the social sciences, theology too can be divided into a wide range of disciplines: biblical studies, church history, systematic theology, and practical theology etc. As a textually oriented discipline, however, theology as a whole is an interpretive discipline. The central question for theological work is to understand the various sources of Christian faith with the aim of clarifying the meaning and implication of Christian faith. As an interpretative discipline theology not only asks: who or what is God? but also: who or what is God for us, in our time? Consequently, the same question facing the social sciences arises here too: in what way does this interpretation take place? In fact, several theologians have given significant contributions to the development of hermeneutics, and the German theologian Friederich Schleiermacher is considered one of the founders of hermeneutics. Further, theology too is a critical discipline. Theology makes text and tradition the object of analysis and is based on the assumption that an analysis of these texts can help one in saying something about Christian faith. However, theology also questions the conditions and prerequisites for speaking about God and adopts a critical attitude toward its sources.

Theology also shares with the social sciences an interest in the contemporary and in both cases, change invites new research. For the social sciences change implies new social realities. The object of study changes and this in turn gives reason to do new empirical studies and to develop new theories relevant for the present. For theology, new social developments imply that the perspective changes. Compared to their predecessors theologians of today have a different position and perspective: today's theologians carry different baggage and a different interpretative framework in their approach to, and interpretation of, the biblical texts, and the Christian faith. Thus a new reading of both the Old and New Testament is required and a renewed reflection on the contemporary meaning and implication of Christian faith.

The contemporary interest in theology is, however, more than a contemporary reading of ancient texts or a new interpretation of God from a new perspective. The question of what or who God is, concerns not only a description of a transcendent phenomenon. There is a contemporary and normative dimension to the question, namely in the question of what such a God and the belief in him or her does for people—individuals and groups—today. In this way, the question of God leads theologians to question people's relationship to themselves and to others in their everyday lives and in times of crisis.

INTERDISCIPLINARY CONNECTIONS

Often theology and the social sciences adopt different approaches. The social scientist works "as if" human life is socially determined, while the theologian works "as if" God exists and works in the world.[14] It is not the case, however, that theology only discusses transcendental realities and life after death, while the social sciences deal with the present world.[15] Importantly, theology seeks not only to understand religious experiences—that is, specifically spiritual or Christian experiences—but also human experiences in the real world. Theology interprets human experience and these are the very same experiences that the social sciences make their study object. This constitutes an obvious interface between theology and social sciences. Human experiences are the focus of both disciplines.

Accordingly, it is misleading to talk about the social sciences as empirical, while theology is not, or to argue that theology is normative while the social sciences are descriptive. Theology and social science are both

14. Gill, *Social Context of Theology*.
15. Berger and Luckmann, *Social Construction of Reality*.

empirical and normative, and both are academic disciplines with related critical and constructive characteristics. They interpret the social reality, criticize it, and give normative direction for constructive action. Consequently, theology and the social sciences overlap and share a number of interdisciplinary connections.

In fact, and although the social sciences have traditionally not been theology's primary partner, significant changes have taken place in this regard. Theologians in particular have been increasingly interested in the relationship between theology and sociology both in principle and in the sense that they have used sociological concepts, methods, and analysis tools in their own theological work. In particular with regard to Christianity's historical growth and the hermeneutical problem of the meaning of texts by charting the social context in which they were produced, sociological perspectives have enriched the scholarly debates.

In the 1960s and -70s neo-Marxism appealed to a number of theologians who in turn made social analysis a constituent part of theological work and liberation theology emerged as a new way of combining theology and social analysis. Liberation theology was linked to ecclesiastical processes, especially the Second Vatican Council from 1962 to 1965 and its openness towards the modern world. Drawing on such resources, liberation theology provided a theology and religiously based social analysis from the perspective of the poor and marginalized. This combination of theologically and socially informed analysis remains a trademark of contemporary liberation theology as well as political theology. Another example can be found in empirical theology, for example in works by Johannes A. van der Ven,[16] Randolph Crump Miller,[17] and others.[18]

Although scholars of sociology of religion[19] are often closer to sociology than to academic theology, they too contribute in developing an interface between the disciplines. Further, several scholars are trained in both fields and come across not as representatives of one of the disciplines exclusively, but rather as reflective practitioners of cross-disciplinary academic work. Three key contributions in this category are Milbank's *Theology and Social*

---

16. Ven, *Practical Theology* and Ven and Scherer-Rath, *Normativity*.

17. Miller, *Empirical Theology*.

18. For more on sociology and theology, see Martin, *Reflections on Sociology and Theology*; Martin, Mills, and Pickering, *Sociology and Theology*; Brewer, "Sociology and Theology Reconsidered"; Gill, *Sociological Theology*; and Nowers and Medina, *Theology*.

19. McGuire, *Religion* and Furseth and Repstad, *Introduction*.

Theory: Beyond Secular Reason,[20] the edited volume *Theology and Sociology: A Reader*[21] and *Theology and the Social Sciences*.[22] Similarly, as theologians have drawn from the social sciences, there has to some extent been a renewed sociological interest in the growth of the Christian church.[23] This contributes to a certain rapprochement between the disciplines.

There is, however, still reason to maintain important distinctions between theology and social sciences. The methodological atheism[24] or methodological agnosticism[25] of the social sciences is one such difference and refers to the issue of God's existence, the truth of religion, etc., but it falls outside the interests and competence of the social scientist to make theological claims. Theological resources, interests, theories, and concepts are different from those widely used in the social sciences.

Further, a strong and influential criticism of this way of understanding this relationship has been articulated, by among others John Milbank.[26] He rejects the understanding of sociology as methodological agnostic, but argues it is outright atheist and rooted in a meta-narrative that simply conflicts with the Christian faith. Thus this represents a full-blown atheist approach to society and an interpretation and understanding of social life. To Milbank, therefore, there is not only a split between theology and social theory, but there are two conflicting world views at play, with profound implications for the interpretations they offer. The two cannot be combined. One must be chosen at the expense of the other. Accordingly, Milbank seeks to defend theology against 'secular reason' and speaks of a "Christian sociology."[27]

On the other hand, all major world religions seems to have a lot to say about social life and, as William Keenan points out, it can be argued that sociology seems trapped in "a secular humanist conceptual net"[28] and is in need of a "theological ear."[29] Keenan argues this would be enormously help-

---

20. Milbank, *Theology and Social Theory*.
21. Gill, *Theology and Sociology*.
22. Barnes, *Theology and the Social Sciences*.
23. Stark, *Rise of Christianity*.
24. Berger, *Sacred Canopy*.
25. Furseth and Repstad, *Introduction*.
26. Milbank, *Theology and Social Theory*.
27. Ibid.
28. Keenan, "Rediscovering," 33.
29. Ibid., 20.

ful to sociologists and could contribute to developing not only theological sociology and sociological theology, but also to a post-secular sociology. Indeed, the postmodern and post-secular turn to deconstruction of biblical hermeneutics and sociological theory "seem to blur the boundaries between all disciplines"[30] and thus represents a new opportunity for both theology and the social sciences. In an applied, practical manner the kairos documents make use of this opportunity.

SOCIAL ANALYSIS IN TIMES OF CRISIS

To sum up, kairos theology emerges from contexts of conflict and oppression. Its social analysis focuses on the suffering and injustice people experience in their everyday lives and is driven by a need to disclose the underlying and pervasive conflict that permeates all parts of social life. The critical assessment of the conflict situation creates sharp contrasts. There is black and white and little room for grey, and the kairos authors reject neutrality, impartiality, and paralysis. In addition, the related divisions or conflict lines that run through the church and the various denominations, are, in the kairos documents, seen as a problem and as a starting point for a critical discussion of the basis function and character of church and theology in society.

This social analysis that is such an integrated part of kairos theology is clearly descriptive. Key paragraphs in the documents and the very starting point of these specific documents and kairos theology in general is a description of the social realities. The social analysis seeks to clarify and interpret the quality, characteristics, fundamental features, and conflicts of our time and in contemporary society. This is a critical task that deals with contemporary issues and seeks to go beyond superficial descriptions and causal explanations in order to identify the problems, structures, and characteristics of society. This is also a normative analysis in the sense that the social analysis is framed and defined by its focus on conflict between oppressors and oppressed and that this is regarded as an unjust relationship that demands a proper response. Indeed, kairos theology highlights social conflicts and the inequality, injustice, and suffering that these cause and is committed to the poor and marginalized, and giving voice to the voiceless.

In other words, the kairos authors are concerned about the root causes of these conflicts and call for these to be addressed, but equally focus on

30. Burdziej, "Sociological and Theological Imagination," 186.

their social, political, and economic consequences. There is an explicit empirical focus on "the reality" and "what is happening" giving priority to the experiences of the poor and marginalized. This leads to a call to take a stand, and a call to those who have chosen the wrong side, to convert. This also implies that the kairos authors reject seeing the current situation and prevailing living conditions as an expression of the divine will. They regard their contexts and crises as historically conditioned, not divinely sanctioned.

The kairos documents thus offer reflections that are both theological and sociological. These perspectives are not presented as distinct separate components, but as part of one integrated whole. The distinction between theology and social theory is hardly made, but rather blurred in a postmodern manner. Accordingly, the two are integrated in a way foreign both to "methodological atheism" and Milbank's notion of a Christian social theory. The kairos authors not only combine theological insights and perspectives with a social analysis rooted in the social sciences, but fuse them in a creative fashion. This gives the theologically informed contribution to the public sphere not only credibility, but also a novel and creative dimension.

A public theology inspired by kairos theology adopts this kind of empirical focus, yet is normatively committed to social analysis and an integrated, innovative, and interdisciplinary approach to the challenges of the day. This implies identifying the key conflicts, the oppressors, and the oppressed and to name the conflict and the implications it has on those who suffer: the poor, marginalized, and oppressed. The contributions of public theology must reflect this kind of positioned analysis. However, while stating this analysis as clearly as possible, public theology should also express the conditions and premises for its social analysis, and thus its limits and tentative character. This implies inviting questions and comments, as well as alternative interpretations and understandings of the crisis at hand and related social issues.

6

Politics and Ethics

Public theology not only provides a description and analysis of social conditions, but must also say something about what needs to be done. It must be critical, constructive, and practical. The question: How can we read the signs of the times? is accompanied by a normative challenge: What should we do? What is it that we must accept, and what should be challenged and changed? What kind of actions and policies should be chosen? This is the problem of politics and ethics in public theology.

In this chapter I will address this problem by outlining how kairos theology deals with political and ethical issues. Drawing on perspectives from Christian ethics, Robert Benne's notion of the "core vision" of the church, as well as the concept of middle axioms, I then discuss how policy implications and moral actions can and should be part of public theology in times of crisis.

HOPE

Focusing on inequality, injustice, suffering, and oppression, the kairos documents present a sharp criticism of society, but this situation is not seen as inevitable or unavoidable. The documents are characterized by a strong belief in the possibility of change and their social analysis is closely followed by a message of hope.

The South African authors believe in "true peace and true reconciliation" (KSA 4.5) and emphasize that one should "act with hope and confidence" (KSA 5.6). Similarly, *The Road to Damascus* articulates a "cry of pain and protest" (RD 42), but rejects the *"denial of all hope for the future"* (RD 52, original emphasis). The authors write:

> This proclamation was written and signed to give an account of the hope that is in us. Like the disciples who travelled along the road to Emmaus we are sometimes tempted to give up hope. As the two disciples say: "Our own hope had been that he (Jesus) would be the one to set Israel free" *(Lk 24:21)*. What they still had to learn from Jesus and what we need to be reminded of again and again is that the way to freedom and salvation is the way of the cross. "Was it not ordained that the Christ should suffer and so enter into his glory?" *(Lk 24:26)*. There is no cheap solution or liberation. There is no easy road. (RD Conclusion, original emphasis)

Kairos Palestine also is a strong witness and commitment to a hope anchored in the Christian faith. Having accounted for the Israeli occupation and the contemporary social conditions in Palestine, the authors write:

> Despite this, our hope remains strong, because it is from God. God alone is good, almighty and loving and his goodness will one day be victorious over the evil in which we find ourselves. As Saint Paul said: *"If God is for us, who is against us? (...) Who will separate us from the love of Christ? Will hardship, or distress, or persecution, or famine, or nakedness, or peril, or sword? As it is written, "For your sake we are being killed all day long" (...) For I am convinced that (nothing) in all creation, will be able to separate us from the love of God"* (Rom 8:31, 35, 36, 39). (KP 3.1, original emphasis)

Later in *Kairos Palestine* it is asserted that "the Resurrection is the source" (KP 3.5) of this hope which is explained as threefold: 1) belief in God, 2) expectation for a better future, and 3) realism (KP 3.2). The concept of hope is thus closely related to "the Kingdom of God" (KP 3.4.2) which is not an earthly kingdom and thus cannot be confined to a particular period in time. This is not to say, however, that hope in the kairos documents simply refers to a future utopia. When the Palestinian church leaders explain the hope they proclaim, they stress this "means not chasing after illusions—we realize that release is not close at hand" (KP 3.2). It is active resistance and realism, not naivety or idealism, which characterizes *Kairos Palestine*.

This hope is nourished by the "signs of hope" (KP 3.3) that the Palestinian authors find in parish communities (KP 3.3), in "local centres of theology" (KP 3.3.1), meetings for inter-religious dialogue (KP 3.3.2), and the "steadfastness of the generations, the belief in the justice of their cause and the continuity of memory, which does not forget the "Nakba" (catastrophe) and its significance" (KP 3.3.3). *Kairos Palestine* also highlights how hope is reflected in "the developing awareness among many Churches throughout the world and their desire to know the truth about what is going on here" (KP 3.3.3). Thus, hope recognizes this-worldly suffering and oppression as well as resistance against this. In short, hope means "not giving in to evil" (KP 3.2).

RESPONSIBILITY TO RESIST

The social analysis of the kairos documents leads the authors to criticize both government inaction and implemented policies. In fact, these documents articulate a profound conflict between the poor and marginalized on the one hand, and the government and political authorities on the other hand. Following their social analysis, *Kairos South Africa* describes the South African government as an "enemy of the people" and "irreformable" (KSA 4.4). The authors find that "[a]ny reform that it might try to introduce would not be calculated to serve the common good but to serve the interests of the minority from whom it received its mandate" (KSA 4.4). The authors also write: "A regime that is in principle the enemy of the people cannot suddenly begin to rule in the interests of all the people" (KSA 4.4).

The kairos authors are aware of the longstanding theological discussions on how Christians should relate to worldly authorities and the relationship between church and state. The theological reflection on this issue relates in particular to the interpretation of Rom 13:1–7, and *Kairos South Africa* quotes the full text from Paul's letter to the Romans:

> You must all obey the governing authorities. Since all government comes from God, the civil authorities were appointed by God. And so anyone who resists authority is rebelling against God's decision, and such an act is bound to be punished. Good behavior is not afraid of magistrates; only criminals have anything to fear. If you want to live without being afraid of authority, you must live honestly and authority may even honor you. The State is there to serve God for your benefit. If you break the law, however, you may

well have fear: the bearing of the sword has its significance. The authorities are there to serve God: they carry out God's revenge by punishing wrongdoers. You must obey, therefore, not only because you are afraid of being punished, but also for conscience's sake. This is also the reason why you must pay taxes, since all government officials are God's officers. They serve God by collecting taxes. Pay every government official what he has a right to ask—whether it be direct tax or indirect, fear or honor. (Rom 13:1–7) (KSA 2.1)[1]

Commenting on this passage *Kairos South Africa* stresses that "in the rest of the Bible God does not demand obedience to oppressive rulers" (KSA 2.1). Moreover, with reference to the empires addressed in the Book of Daniel and the Book of Revelations, the authors argue that "God *allowed* them to reign for a while but he did not *approve* of what they did. It was not God's will. His will was the freedom and liberation of Israel. Rom 13:1–7 cannot be contradicting all of this" (KSA 2.1, original emphasis).

Romans 13 is also highlighted in *The Road to Damascus*. The authors write:

> The famous text from Romans 13 is misused to demand unquestioning and uncritical allegiance to the political authorities who exercise the politics of death and deception. Similarly, in some countries Christians are commanded to submit themselves blindly to the absolute authority of church leaders. (RD 66)

By identifying the misuse of Romans 13 and rejecting blind obedience to authority, political authority, or church leaders, *The Road to Damascus* justifies its political criticism. Similarly, the authors of *Kairos Palestine* write:

> Our Church points to the Kingdom, which cannot be tied to any earthly kingdom. Jesus said before Pilate that he was indeed a king but *"my kingdom is not from this world"* (Jn 18:36). Saint Paul says: *"The Kingdom of God is not food and drink but righteousness and peace and joy in the Holy Spirit"* (Rom 14:17). Therefore, religion cannot favor or support any unjust political regime, but must rather promote justice, truth and human dignity. It must exert every effort to purify regimes where human beings suffer injustice and human dignity is violated. The Kingdom of God on earth is not dependent on any political orientation, for it is greater and more

---

1. In a footnote the authors remark that this quote is from the Jerusalem Bible. Readers are encouraged to compare this with other translations.

inclusive than any particular political system. (KP 3.4.3, original emphasis)

The kairos authors thus not only argue in favor of theo-political criticism, but identify the theological commitment to "justice, truth, and human dignity" beyond "any particular political system." In this way, they place their political engagement outside and beyond the boundaries of contemporary party politics. It is an engagement driven by Christian faith, moral values, and a normative commitment to the well-being of all.

RECONCILIATION, JUSTICE, AND LOVE

In both the South African and the Palestinian documents the conflict centered analysis is followed by a discussion of the desirability of reconciliation. Reconciliation is not dismissed, but in both cases it has important conditions attached. In *Kairos South Africa* one key condition is a "radical change of structures" (KSA 3.2). The document speaks of "reform-justice" that should be replaced with a "more radical justice that comes from below and is determined by the people of South Africa" (KSA 3.2). This justice is understood as a "common good of *all the people*" (KSA 4.4, original emphasis) and, accordingly, the document distinguishes between peace and "true peace," reconciliation and "true reconciliation" (KSA 4.5). True peace and true reconciliation include justice. Reconciliation cannot be rightfully conceived without justice. Similarly, the Palestinian authors "see a determination among many to overcome the resentments of the past and to be ready for reconciliation once justice has been restored" (KP 3.3.4), thus making reconciliation dependent on justice.

A similar concern is evident in the way that the kairos authors elaborate their understanding of love. In *Kairos Palestine* love is explained as "seeing the face of God in every human being" (KP 4.2.1), invoking the notion of all human beings being created in the image of God (Gen 1). The thrust of this understanding of love lies in its strong insistence that "love seeks to correct the evil and stop the aggression (. . .) by walking in the ways of justice" (KP 4.2.1). Against those who reject the political involvement of churches and Christians, it is argued that: "Resistance is a right and a duty for the Christian. But it is resistance with love as its logic" (KP 4.2.3), which implies "[s]eeing the image of God in the face of the enemy" (KP 4.2.3).

In this way, the kairos documents establish strong links between concepts that often are considered conflicting or contradictory: reconciliation and justice as well as love and resistance: "Resistance to the evil of occupation is integrated, then, within this Christian love that refuses evil and corrects it" (KP 4.2.5). This is the socio-theological starting point for the constructive and practical elements in the kairos documents. The Palestinian church leaders write they "bear the strength of love rather than that of revenge, a culture of life rather than a culture of death. This is a source of hope for us, for the Church and for the world" (KP 3.4.5). Similarly, the connectedness between opponents in the contemporary conflict, friends and enemies, is stressed: "Through our love, we will overcome injustices and establish foundations for a new society both for us and for our opponents. Our future and their future are one" (KP 4.3).

BOYCOTT, DIVESTMENT, AND VIOLENCE

In addition to a general call for justice and resistance with the logic of love, the kairos authors outline actions that specifically target the suffering and oppressed. For example, they explicitly defend the need to exercise civil disobedience and suggest concrete and effective actions. In this way, they move beyond abstract principles expressed in terms of love, justice, and reconciliation and towards a more context-sensitive, applied, and policy relevant normative analysis.

Given the theological character of the kairos documents, it is not surprising that they explicitly address the actions churches and Christians should take in response to the kairos they are facing. In fact, the recommended actions in *Kairos South Africa* are firstly the traditional forms of ecclesiastical actions such as baptism, worship services, etc. This mirrors the authors' church affiliation and a close connection between spirituality and social action. Similarly, *Kairos Palestine* includes a reflection on "the mission of the Church" (KP 3.4) which is defined as "prayer and service [which] is prophetic, bearing the voice of God in the present and the future" (KP 3.4). The church is understood as a "people who pray and serve" (KP 3.4) who side with "the oppressed" (KP 3.4.1). The Palestinian authors find that they are "called to pray and to make our voice heard" (KP 3.4.2) and reject "silencing the prophetic voice given by the Spirit to the Churches" (KP 5.2). The prophetic aspect of this mission is explained as a calling to "speak the Word of God courageously, honestly and lovingly in the local context and in the midst of daily events" (KP 3.4.1). The church is called to follow Jesus' example in standing "by the side of each poor person and each sinner, calling them to repentance, life, and the restoration of the dignity bestowed on them by God" (KP 3.4.1).

In particular *Kairos Palestine* discusses a wide range of actions. One example is the call on the international community to change its policies with regard to the Israeli-Palestinian conflict. The authors appeal to the international community to "stop the principle of "double standards" and insist on the international resolutions regarding the Palestinian problem with regard to all parties" (KP 7). They argue that the international community practices "[s]elective application of international law" and that this "legitimizes the claims by certain armed groups and states that the international community only understands the logic of force" (KP 7). More specifically *Kairos Palestine* suggests sanctions and "divestment and an economic and commercial boycott of everything produced by the occupation" (KP 4.2.6). Boycott and divestment are understood as "tools of non violence for justice, peace and security for all" (KP 6.3). The boycott is intended as a means of achieving a positive goal of the best "for all," but is geared specifically towards Israel (KP 7).

It is worth noting how this recommendation of boycott comes with emphasis on non-violent opposition and peaceful ways to solve the conflict and how it is stressed that "this is not revenge" (KP 7). However, one of the areas where the kairos documents have differing conclusions is the question of violence. *Kairos Palestine* rejects violent resistance. The primary concern is to defend the right to resist the Israeli occupation, but non-violence is given a particularly central role. The authors believe "[t]he ways of force must give way to the ways of justice" (KP 4.2.2), find they "cannot resist evil with evil" (KP 4.2.4) and therefore suggest resisting through civil disobedience (KP 4.2.5).

The South African document, on the other hand, rejects non-violence as an absolute principle. Considering the context and the current situation, the authors conclude that such an "absolute principle [would be] simply counter-productive" (KSA 3.3). They reject an abstract approach to "anything anyone *calls* violence without regard for who is using it, which side they are on or what purpose they have in mind" (KSA 3.3, original emphasis). They argue that "[t]o call all physical force 'violence' is to try to be neutral and to refuse to make a judgement about who is right and who is wrong" (KSA 3.3). The South African authors also point out that resistance

Politics and Ethics

to the status quo can be violent, and that they are already experiencing what they call structural violence. By this they mean "the structural, institutional and unrepentant violence of the State and especially the oppressive and naked violence of the police and the army" (KSA 3.3). Accordingly, and in contrast to *Kairos Palestine*, the South African document defends violence in situations (under restrictive circumstances) that require "physical force to defend oneself against aggressors and tyrants" (KSA 3.3).[2]

CHRISTIAN ETHICS

With these reflections and recommendations the kairos authors make the implications of their social analysis explicit and specify what they imply for politicians, religious groups, and individuals. In this way, they show how kairos theology not only expresses Christian faith and theology, but also Christian, practical, and political ethics. In doing so, they also position kairos theology in relation to other approaches to Christian faith, ethics, and political involvement.

Christian faith is not only, not even primarily, about ethics, but it does offer perspectives and resources for ethical reflection. Neither biblical texts nor Christian ethics prescribe, however, ready-made answers to current social or political issues, but these come as a result of the interpretations and considered judgement of the Christian community or the individual Christian. This brings Christian ethics close to public theology. In fact, in his discussion of the nature of public theology, Breitenberg concludes that "public theology is most closely related to what is often called public or social ethics; that is, Christian public theology is more like Christian public or social ethics than it is the other areas."[3]

As an academic field Christian ethics is often divided into categories such as deontological ethics, consequential or utilitarian ethics, and virtue ethics, divine command ethics etc. Samuel Wells and Ben Quash make a different categorization and speak of universal ethics, subversive ethics, and ecclesial ethics. These are characterized as being ethics for anyone, ethics for the excluded and ethics for the church respectively.[4] All these

---

2. For more on the South African debate on theology and violence, see Villa-Vicencio, *Theology and Violence*.

3. Breitenberg, "To Tell the Truth," 62. See also Graham and Reed, *Future of Christian Social Ethics*; Biggar, *Behaving in Public*; and Gushee, *In the Fray*.

4. Wells and Quash, *Introducing Christian Ethics*.

distinctions indicate the pluralism that exists within the field of Christian ethics. Interestingly, kairos theology both reflects and adds to this pluralism, but cannot be easily placed in any of these categories. The discussion of injustice, oppression, and division within the church reflects Christian pluralism on political and ethical issues, but by taking a stand and offering policy recommendations and suggesting specified moral actions, the kairos authors add to the same pluralism.

Another dimension of the scholarly discussions on the character of Christian ethics is the distinction between the private and the public. Influenced by modernity, individualism, secularization, and pietism, some have argued that Christian ethics primarily relates to the private sphere. Christian ethics is about the life of the individual Christian and the choices he or she makes in life. The fields of public policy and politics are considered beyond the scope of religious ethics. Such arguments have come from both within the faith community and from people positioned outside it. They have emphasized the independence of politics and the uniqueness of political processes compared to that of the individuals lives in their small scale homes and families.

Bonhoeffer has famously challenged those who wish to limit their ethical reflections and judgements to the private sphere and thus withdraw from politics. He writes:

> Some who seek to escape from taking a stand publicly find a place of refuge in a *private virtuousness*. Such a man does not steal. He does not commit murder. He does not commit adultery. Within the limits of his powers he does good. But in his voluntary renunciation of publicity he knows how to remain punctiliously within the permitted bounds which preserve him from involvement in conflict. He must be blind and deaf to the wrongs which surround him. It is only at the price of an act of self-deception that he can safeguard his private blamelessness against contamination through responsible action in the world.[5]

As shown, kairos theology similarly dismisses this privatized or individualistic understanding of Christian ethics and in addressing public issues, Christian ethics and kairos theology become normative and applied. As normative ethics it discusses what is right, wrong, good or bad in specific cases, and as applied ethics it addresses particular practices and cases.

---

5. Bonhoeffer, *Ethics*, 69.

THE CORE VISION

One important starting point for many theologians and church leaders when reflecting on the political role of churches and other Christian actors has been the understanding of the church as an institution (relatively) independent from the state. This independence can, however, be interpreted in two different directions. On the one hand it can be understood as a platform for freedom to criticize the state. On the other hand, when the Church is seen as separated from the State and the political sphere, it can also be seen as politically inept. Church based involvement in politics can be rejected on the basis of lack of competence.

Benne's understanding of these issues is illustrative. In his discussion of public theology for the twenty-first century he argues that the essential mission of the church is to proclaim the gospel and that it "must attend to its core vision, not only proclaiming it, but attempting to be faithful to it in all its practices and endeavors."[6] By core vision he means "the event of Jesus as the Christ," surrounded by "the biblical and early church's witness to the events of Jesus' life, death, and resurrection" and summarized in the ecumenical creeds.[7] Not part of the core itself, but "closely related" to it, is "the central moral vision of the Christian faith."[8]

Benne describes this core vision and the moral vison of the Christian faith as two inner orbs at the center of three concentric circles. The closest concentric circle is what he calls "the more speculative theological reflections of the church, including its social teachings," meaning "the efforts of the church to apply its religious and moral vision to the dynamic world around it. These efforts entail significant steps in moving from the core vision to its application to specific problems."[9] The next concentric circle represents "the church's posture on specific public policy issues," and Benne argues such "specific commitments on the part of the church ought generally to be quite infrequent" although "in special times with regard to special issues, the church may have to stand for or against them."[10]

Benne finds that each of these concentric circles represents a challenge to the church and the Christian community. He writes:

---

6. Benne, *Paradoxical Vision*, 72.
7. Ibid., 72–73.
8. Ibid., 73.
9. Ibid., 73–74.
10. Ibid., 74.

> It is essential that the church is able to distinguish these different circles and to hold their contents with differing degrees of commitment and passion. The central religious and moral visions ought to be held with clarity, confidence and steadfastness. They have the highest degree of authority and consensus in the church. The outer circles are much more susceptible to genuine and permissible disagreement. Moreover, as one moves toward the outer circles, the church has less and less warrant and knowledge for pronouncing or acting upon its judgments.[11]

In contrast, kairos theology makes a much closer connection between theological reflection and social analysis. Indeed, they are distinguished neither in a temporal way nor as different circles that can be held "with differing degrees of commitment and passion." Rather, theology and social analysis go hand in hand and are integrated into one and the same theo-political statement. The "core vision" is not purely doctrinal or moral, but encompasses a critical social analysis and practical commitments to specific public policy issues. In short, where Benne draws distinctions, kairos theology makes connections. In kairos theology the social and political positioning of the church expresses and interprets its faith and theology. Faith and action are seen as closely intertwined.

CREDIBILITY AND AUTHORITY

With regard to the action component of public theology, Benne distinguishes between institutional and individual engagement. The first is exemplified by the social pronouncements made by churches on human rights, legislation etc. Individual engagement takes place when Christians "become active agents for the values of that tradition in their worldly roles in economics, politics and culture."[12] Against this background, Benne develops a typology of four models for interaction between religion and public life as he distinguishes between indirect and direct interaction and intentional and unintentional actions.

The indirect form of interaction implies that the institutional church refrains from doing public theology, although it might still influence the public sphere and public life through the laity or affiliated organizations. This influence can be unintentional, meaning that "the church has no

---

11. Ibid., 74.
12. Ibid., 9.

definite, conscious intent to affect its public environment in a particular direction."[13] Benne argues that this:

> indirect and unintentional influence approach seems to fit the traditional doctrine of the church's mission. It focuses on the central calling of the church, the preaching of the gospel, and confines its main activities to the formation of its members in the core religious and moral values of its vision. Furthermore, this approach does not bestow authority on the church to claim more competence and spend more energy on issues peripheral to its central mission.[14]

As implied, the indirect approach can also be combined with an intentional strategy to engage in public life. This is the case when churches refrain from becoming public actors themselves, but still encourage their individual members to make such direct connections in their own capacities. The role of the church is not to issue political statements, but rather to:

> encourage genuine religious moral reflection among its laity. This would take the kind of care and restraint that is rare among the churches but would be well worth the effort. It would make for well-formed and informed laity who could make effective connections between their religious tradition and the public world.[15]

When the interaction is more direct, the church as an institution seeks to engage society, for example through the issuing of formal institutional statements and actions. It is worth noting, however, that Benne concludes his discussion of direct and intentional influence with several cautionary notes. He argues that "[c]hurch statements first of all should be directed to their internal constituencies," that "[w]hen it is not necessary for the church to speak, it is necessary for the church not to speak" and, finally, that "when the church does speak, it ought to make sure that it is speaking with the authentic voice of its own tradition."[16]

Benne is, in other words, very cautious about the role of the church as a direct participant in the public sphere. In circumstances when it is necessary for the church to speak out, he highlights, however, the need to

---

13. Ibid., 184.
14. Ibid., 189–90.
15. Ibid., 194.
16. Ibid., 214–15.

speak "in its own tradition." This is related to the credibility of the church. Credibility, Benne argues:

> increases as the frequency of church social statements decreases. (. . .) . . .the church should practice great restraint in addressing society. Restraint follows from two realizations: first, that the church's primary mission is not to instruct society on how it is to be ordered and, second, that its competence to do so effectively is severely limited. (. . .) Similarly, the church should speak only when it has something unique to offer from its own theological-ethical heritage.[17]

In this context Benne stresses the importance of "the bearers of the tradition" when articulating and explicating the church's corporate conscience, but he also points out the need for interdisciplinary cooperation: "Certainly these bearers of tradition must listen to expert opinion from secular authorities in the field, from those involved in the issue, and from those whose interest or person is harmed by social injustice."[18] Indeed, he stresses that church statements of this kind demand thorough preparation and considered judgement.

Finally, Benne argues that credibility is also strengthened by the weight of authority, be it the (Catholic) magisterium, church assemblies, or bishops. In this context he also underlines the need to distinguish between different levels of authority. He argues that the symbols of redemption and the ethical principles that follow from these constitute the highest level of authority and, indeed, correspond to what he refers to as the church's core vision. Statements on particular political issues have a lower level of authority. Illustrative examples (from the 1970s and -80s) are, according to Benne, found in the Catholic Church's support of Solidarity, the preferential option for the poor in Latin American liberation theology, Protestant support for democratic movements in South Korea and East Germany, and the World Council of Churches' support of various liberation organizations in southern Africa. He argues:

> Such direct actions threaten to instrumentalize and secularize the sacred symbols of the church in pursuit of very secular, partisan agendas. The church loses its needed distance from all political action; its claim to point to transcendence collapses if it draws too close to a political program of action. Consequently it has a

17. Ibid., 207.
18. Ibid.

more difficult time proclaiming a universal gospel to all repentant sinners regardless of what side of the political fence they are on. Certainly this has been a tendency of all churches too closely allied to political authority and too deeply involved in political power.[19]

Benne proposes two guidelines to limit churches' involvement in this kind of direct action. Firstly, he argues it is:

> far more important to call attention to an injustice or social evil than to prescribe or even support legislative measures to address it. (. . .) [T]he church should speak proscriptively, not prescriptively. The church should use whatever moral weight it has to point powerfully to the presence of great challenges to our society.
>
> Given the ambiguous effects of even the best legislation, however, it is prudent for the church to let policy makers shape legislation. The church can provide a further service if it is able to reflect critically on all legislation from its perspective, drawing out the pros and cons as it sees them. Only in rare cases of great clarity should the church actually support particular policy proposals.[20]

Secondly, he argues that churches should focus on extremes but leave the middle ground alone. He writes:

> Great evils and great goods should be the focus of public sector advocacy. The church should be able to bring its prophetic concerns to bear on behalf of those persons who are experiencing great suffering. The church will be most effective at this task if it can speak of that suffering firsthand from its ministry to suffering persons. Likewise, the church should provide a vision of the common good that is both hopeful and realistic, but it should not purport to identify the particular policies that will contribute to that vision.[21]

With these guidelines and recommendations the contrast between Benne's approach and that of kairos theology becomes evident. While Benne wants church involvement in politics to be limited to rare cases, extreme positions, and expressed proscriptively rather than prescriptively, kairos theology finds that even "normal times" are characterized by conflicts that amount to crisis. This results in suffering and oppression for some and makes it necessary to challenge status quo. This is a challenge to all and a task for churches and Christians to identify and address such conflicts

19. Ibid., 217.
20. Ibid., 221–22.
21. Ibid., 222.

and injustices. Further, Benne makes the point that there are some issues that are peripheral to the church's mission and argues against the sacralization of disputed policy issues. Clearly, the kairos authors take a different view. Not only do they place moral policy matters firmly at the center of Christian theology, they do not hesitate to articulate this perspective in the public sphere and in relation to political issues.

Further, the kairos authors share Benne's concern that the church should speak "with the authentic voice of its own tradition" and might also agree that the church should not speak when it is not necessary to speak. Importantly, however, the kairos authors find themselves in times of crisis, a situation that calls on them to cry out in pain, speak truth to power, resist, and act responsibly. Benne's exceptional cases are their status quo.

As the kairos documents are not official church documents, they belong to Benne's category of indirect forms of action where the institutional church refrains from making its own public statements. However, kairos theology does not make the same distinction between churches and Christians that Benne relies on, but call on both groups to reflect on the social and political implications of the Christian faith and to act accordingly. Kairos theology also rejects the distinction Benne makes between proscriptive and prescriptive statements, as well as the notion that abstract principles have higher authority than particular policy proposals. Rather, these concrete recommendations suggest the practical implications of the Christian faith in a given context and crisis.

MIDDLE AXIOMS

While Benne is skeptical about churches' involvement in particular policies, the so-called middle axiom approach adopts a much more positive and constructive attitude this issue. This approach aims at making Christian ethics and public theology informed by and relevant to politicians, policy makers, and other practitioners when faced with their many political and moral dilemmas of practical political decision making.

The middle axiom approach is intimately linked to the work of the Scottish missionary and ecumenical pioneer, J. H. Oldham. He defined middle axioms as something:

> between purely general statements of the ethical demands of the gospel and the decisions that have to be made in concrete situations there is need for what may be described as middle axioms. It

Politics and Ethics

is these that give relevance and point to the Christian ethic. They are attempts to define the directions in which, in a particular state of society, Christian faith must express itself. They are not binding for all time, but are provisional definitions of the type of behaviour of Christians in a given period and given circumstances.[22]

In this Oldham follows Temple who had argued that "the Church must denounce Christian utopianism and confine its attention to realistic possibilities."[23] This comes about through dialogue and interdisciplinary cooperation. Ronald H. Preston drew on both Temple and Oldham and reinterpreted this line of thinking in his:

> insistence upon the essentially dialogical nature of Christian social ethics: that is, that it entails mutually critical and reconstructive engagement between sources and norms of Christian tradition on the one hand, such as Bible and moral theology, and relevant authorities in the social and human sciences.[24]

Accordingly, Preston would consider middle axioms as:

> mediating moral directives that have a key function in Christian moral reasoning in the critical moral ground between the shared beliefs and related ethical principles of Christianity, and the very specific decisions and judgements that Christians as policymakers, practitioners, citizens and voters must be free to make on often complex economic, social and political matters.[25]

In this perspective compromise is the considered, realistic response to conflicting considerations, either between ideal or realistic limitations or between opposing goods or values. From a Catholic perspective John Courtney Murray articulates such an approach already in *We Hold These Truths*,[26] and Miroslav Volf is one of those who continue to insist on the need to recognize realistic limitations. He argues: "Christian communities must learn how to work vigorously for the limited change that is possible, to mourn over persistent and seemingly ineradicable evils, and to celebrate the good wherever it happens and whoever its agents are."[27]

---

22. Quoted in Storrar, "Scottish Civil Society," 38. See Visser 't Hooft and Oldham, *Church and Its Function* and Preston, *Church and Society*.

23. Forrester, "Scope of Public Theology," 13–14.

24. Graham, "Guest Editorial," 2.

25. Storrar, "Scottish Civil Society," 38.

26. Murray, *We Hold These Truths*.

27. Volf, *Public Faith*, 83.

INTERRUPTION AND IMAGINATION

Benne incorporates the middle axioms into his framework for public theology and his critique of church practices. In line with Oldham, Benne finds that "middle principles" are "not binding for all time, but are provisional definitions of the type of behavior required of Christians at a given period and in given circumstances."[28] Benne contrasts such "middle principles" and policy proposals with what he calls a:

> straight-line thinking, in which judgements on particular policies are elevated to the same level as the highest religious symbol—that is, a straight line is drawn in which policy pronouncements are equated with unchanging truth. This is a formula for idolatry, for in it lesser issues are identified with the ultimate.[29]

Benne finds that it is this kind of thinking that has led to what he sees as an "increasing number of calls for *status confessionis* approaches to controversial issues by activist segments in the churches,"[30] both from left-leaning activists and right-wing religious groups. Thus, while Benne is skeptical about the church identifying particular policies, he is positive about the cooperation between churches and theologians on the one hand, and experts and professionals on the other hand.

Others have criticized the middle axiom approach. Koopman argues for a more flexible and inclusive approach, with a stronger narrative component than the middle axioms in particular allows for. He finds that the middle axiom discourse should:

> not only include policymakers, intellectuals and other people with social power, but should include the local knowledge of marginalized people, and the theological and hermeneutical insights of people who do not form part of the academy, civil service, educated elite and politicians.[31]

Another issue Koopman raises is how this kind of approach relates to the preferential option for the poor. He argues that the "notion of the option of the most vulnerable serves as a benchmark with regard to policymaking and especially the adoption of compromises" and that Christian

---

28. Benne, *Paradoxical Vision*, 210.
29. Ibid., 210.
30. Ibid., original emphasis.
31. Koopman, "Churches and Public Policy," 52.

Politics and Ethics

realism and the notion of middle axioms "can only be of use if they heed this preferential option for the poor and marginalized."[32]

Thus, in contrast to Benne's understanding, kairos theology presents itself not as an application of Christian theology on a context, but rather as a theology rooted in, and shaped by, its context. Similarly, in contrast to the key role given to experts and professionals in the middle axiom approach, kairos theology shares Koopman's emphasis on broad, popular participation and the preferential option for the poor. Accordingly, the kairos documents are characterized neither by Benne's core vision nor the realism and compromise oriented middle axiom approach. Rather, in their social analysis the kairos documents reject political compromise in favor of justice for the poor, although in their suggestions for ways of resisting oppression and marginalization, practical action, realism, and a willingness to find pragmatic solutions are also evident. In this sense there seems to be a degree of internal tension within kairos theology, between its radical, prophetic elements on the one hand and its more pragmatic, realistic approach on the other hand.

POLITICS AND ETHICS IN TIMES OF CRISIS

Public theology takes place in the public sphere, and focusses on social and political concerns and challenges. Addressing such issues implies not only contributing to the understanding and interpretation of these concerns. It also involves identifying policy choices and recommending actions and policy implementation. This not only reflects the ties between public, political, and prophetic theologies, but also the moral dimension and applied character of public theology. Against this background, it is not surprising that Christian realism and the middle axiom approach have played an important role in public theology.

Similarly, the kairos documents not only present the utopian, prophetic vision of God's love for everyone, but also point to political means and policy strategies that can be implemented on real-political terms. The theological understanding of these forms of resistance and actions indicates how the moral recommendations are not independent from, but an integrated part of kairos theology. Put differently, they are part of the Christian social ethics of these documents. As such, the public theology of these

---

32. Ibid., 54.

documents does not shy away from general values or theological visions, but also spells out their practical consequences.

However, kairos theology's approach to the problem of politics and ethics in public theology, contrasts with both that of Benne and the middle axiom approach. In contrast to Benne, kairos theology relies on a comprehensive social analysis that identifies the conflicts and problems of the status quo. They argue that this results in suffering and injustice and represents a crisis that requires theological, moral, and practical attention. While Benne is concerned about the limits of public theology, kairos theology points to its necessity. In contrast to the middle axiom approach kairos theology puts a much stronger emphasis on popular participation and the preferential option for the poor. While political compromise is a pragmatic solution in the middle axiom approach, kairos theology is not ready to compromise at the expense of justice or human dignity.

To the kairos authors it is crucial to identify ways of acting and to act in the crisis situation they see themselves in. This is not to distort law or gospel neither does it reduce public theology to a "gospel ethic." It recognizes, however, that a kairos moment is a moment to speak out, to take a stand, and to act. This might also be the weakness of kairos theology. It risks providing simple answers to complex issues. Further, kairos theology rejects an abstract approach to Christian ethics, but does rely on notions or principles of justice, reconciliation, and love when it qualifies its own recommendations and suggestions. The kairos documents do not, however, provide specific answers without regard to context. The documents address specific issues and suggest particular policies in a considered contextual manner. In other words, and as indicated by these documents' differing views on violence, kairos theology is not a fixed program with readymade solutions for the social challenges of our time.

Public theology inspired by kairos theology adopts these applied, normative, and practical features. It becomes the task of public theology not only to identify and interpret the crisis in light of the Christian faith, but also to address the issue of how to respond to the crisis at hand. This takes public theology into the field of politics and policy implementation. At times compromise, middle axioms and cautionary, realistic polices are in place. At other times public theology needs to address the conflict and antagonism at stake, take a stand, and spell out its position.

In other words, one of the inherent problems in public theology is the tension between the prophetic, utopian dimension of public theology and the more realistic, reformist approach based on middle axioms. A kairos inspired public theology retains both perspectives and is articulated in a dynamic tension between the two, giving public theology a challenging and creative character.

7

Language and Voice

In bringing their theologically informed contribution to the public sphere, churches and Christians can translate their religious concerns into a secular and rational language. Alternatively, they explicitly use the language of their particular religious tradition and conviction. This would be a distinctly religious voice. It could rely on religious narratives or it could be distinctly apologetic or prophetic. Given the range of options, how should public theology express its perspectives and concerns? This is the problem of language and voice in public theology.

In this chapter I begin by examining how biblical language and theological terminology is used in kairos theology. I then look more closely at how *Kairos Palestine* discusses the issue of land as God's land. This leads to a discussion on the theological understanding of the Word of God in kairos theology. Against this background, I close the chapter with a discussion of the practice of translation and bilingualism in public theology. I argue that public theology should use a reasonably accessible religious language and speak with a clear and inclusive voice.

BIBLICAL LANGUAGE

The kairos documents present themselves and their concerns in an explicitly religious language. There is an active use of quotes from, and references to, biblical texts. As they discuss oppression, conflict, war, and peace, biblical texts on these topics are highlighted.

Language and Voice

One example of this is *Kairos South Africa*'s emphasis on how the Bible addresses violence and oppression. "Throughout the Bible the word violence is used to describe everything that is done by a wicked oppressor" (KSA 3.3), the authors write. Oppression is interpreted in light of "the many, many vivid and concrete descriptions of suffering and oppression throughout the Bible culminating in the cross of Jesus" (KSA 4.2), and several examples are given:

> First of all it is described as the painful experience of being crushed to the ground: "Yahweh, they crush your people" (Ps 94:5); "We are bowed in the dust, our bodies crushed to the ground" (Ps 44:25); It is the experience of being weighed down by heavy loads (Exod 1:11; Matt 11:28). But it is more than just an experience of being degraded and humiliated. They lived with the terrifying reality of killings and murders. "We are being massacred daily" (Ps 44:22). "Yahweh, they oppress your hereditary people, murdering and massacring widows, orphans and migrants" (Ps 94:5–6). What grief and torment this causes. "My bones are in torment, my soul is in utter torment. I am worn out with groaning, every night I drench my pillow and soak my bed with tears, my eye is wasted with grief; I have grown old with enemies all round me" (Ps 6:3, 6–10). (KSA 4.2)

These and other biblical references are applied to the context and situation of the kairos authors. For example, Nehemiah's witness of slavery in Israel is linked to the current situation in South Africa:

> "Here we are now, enslaved; here in the land you gave our Fathers, we are slaves. Its rich fruits swell the profit of the kings who dispose as they please of our bodies and our cattle" (Neh. 9:36–37). For the people of South Africa this situation is all too familiar. (KSA 4.2)

Kairos South Africa also points out how suffering is a recurring topic in the Bible:

> "The sons of Israel are oppressed" (Jer 50:33); "You will be exploited and crushed continually" (Dt. 28:33). They were oppressed by the tyrannical, imperial nations around them. First it was the Egyptians: "The Egyptians ill-treated us, they gave us no peace and inflicted harsh slavery upon us" (Dt. 26:6). Then the various Canaanite kings oppressed them, for example Jabin the Canaanite king of Hasor "cruelly oppressed the Israelites for twenty years" (Jud 4:3). And so it carried on with the Philistines, the Assyrians,

the Babylonians, the Greeks and the Romans, each in turn exercising an oppressive domination over this small nation. (KSA 4.2)[1]

Similarly, *The Road to Damascus* makes several references to the Bible in its effort to understand and discuss poverty, violence, and oppression: Exod 3:17; Ps 103:6; Luke 1:52; Matt 25:31–46 (RD 40). The document also refers to the biblical prophets, including the biblical discussion of false prophets:

> Beware of false prophets. They come to us disguised as sheep but inside they are wild wolves. We can recognize what they really are by their fruits *(Mt 7:15–20)*. There are false prophets who say there is peace when there is no peace *(Jer 6:14; 8:11; Ez 13:10)*. Hear the prophetic voice of those who are being persecuted and oppressed. (RD 88, original emphasis)

The Road to Damascus also makes several Bible references on idolatry: Rom 1:25; Exod 20:4–5; Ps 115:4; Matt 6:24; and Luke 16:13 (RD 49), as well as John 8:2–11 (RD 54). These texts are applied to current phenomena such as materialism and the consumer society (RD 50). The authors argue:

> Idolatry is the sin of worshipping or being subservient to someone or something which is not God, treating some created thing as if it were a god. "They worshipped and served the creature instead of the Creator" *(Rm 1:25)*. In the Old Testament Moses and the prophets condemned the worship of the golden calf, the Baals and other idols made by human hands *(Ex 20:4–5; Ps 115:4)*. In New Testament times the principal form of idolatry was the worship of mammon *(Mt. 6:24; Lk 16:13)*.
>
> The same is true for us today. In our countries, the worship of money, power, privilege and pleasure has certainly replaced the worship of God. (RD 49–50, original emphasis)

Against this background, the kairos authors call for conversion and again turn to the biblical narrative to explain what this implies:

> The most famous conversion story in the New Testament is the story of the apostle Paul on the road to Damascus. Before his conversion, Saul (as he was then called) persecuted those Jews who had been converted to the way of Jesus. He took sides with the Sanhedrin, the chief priests of the Temple, the scribes and the Pharisees, against Jesus and the people who believed in Jesus. In

---

1. Similar texts that highlight the poor include Luke 1:51–52 (KSA 2.4); Luke 6:20–24; and 4:18 (RD 36).

Language and Voice

> other words, Saul sided with the authorities and the status quo against this new movement that wanted to "turn the world upside down" *(Acts 17:6)*. Saul stood by and approved the killing of Stephen *(Acts 7:58; 8:1)*. Stephen, like Jesus, was seen as a dangerous threat to the Temple and the Law *(Acts 6:14–15)*. (. . .)
>
> "Saul was still breathing threats to slaughter the Lord's disciples" as he travelled down the road to Damascus armed with letters authorizing him to arrest any followers of the Way, men or women, that he could find" *(Acts 9:1–2)*. Then suddenly it happened. Saul made the startling discovery that he was on the wrong side, that God was on the side of Jesus and that the persecution of the people who followed Jesus was the persecution of Jesus himself.
>
> "Saul, Saul, why do you persecute me?
> Who are you, Lord?
> I am Jesus whom you are persecuting" *(Acts 9:3–5)*. (. . .)
>
> Saul became Paul when he accepted in faith that the true God was in Jesus and that the risen Lord was in the very people who he had been persecuting. (RD 83–85, original emphasis)

From this account the kairos authors deduce a general, contemporary call to "be converted again and again from the idol of mammon and the worship of the true God. We cannot serve two masters, we cannot serve both God and mammon *(Mt 6:24)*" (RD 87, original emphasis).

Another important narrative in kairos theology is the exodus story:

> The Lord said: I have seen how my people are suffering as slaves in Egypt, and I have heard them beg for my help because of the way they are being mistreated. I feel sorry for them, and I have come down to rescue them from the Egyptians. I will bring my people out of Egypt into a country where there is good land, rich with milk and honey. I will give them the land where the Canaanites, Hittites, Amorites, Perizzites, Hivites, and Jebusites now live. My people have begged for my help, and I have seen how cruel the Egyptians are to them. Now go to the king! I am sending you to lead my people out of his country. (Exod 3:7–10)[2]

In liberation theology this narrative has had a profound role in expressing God's identification with the oppressed and his or her promise and commitment to free the slaves and deliver us from evil. It seems to serve much the same function in kairos theology and is highlighted in both *Kairos*

---

2. Contemporary English Version (CEV).

INTERRUPTION AND IMAGINATION

South Africa (KSA 3.2) and *The Road to Damascus* (RD 41). *Kairos South Africa* cites Isaiah:

> The Spirit of the Lord has been given to me.
> For he has anointed me.
> He has sent me to bring the good news to the poor,
> To proclaim liberty to captives
> And to the blind new sight,
> To set the downtrodden free
> To proclaim the Lord's year of favor (Lk 4:18–19; KSA 4.5).

Similarly, in *Kairos Palestine* the appeal to love has a long list of references: John 13:34 and Matt 5:45–47 (KP 4.4), as well as Rom 12:17 and 1 Pet 3:9 (KP 4.1). *Kairos Palestine* also quotes 1 Pet 3:15:

> We call on Christians to remain steadfast in this time of trial, just as we have throughout the centuries, through the changing succession of states and governments. Be patient, steadfast and full of hope so that you might fill the heart of every one of your brothers or sisters who shares in this same trial with hope. *"Always be ready to make your defense to anyone who demands from you an accounting for the hope that is in you"* (1 Pet. 3:15). Be active and, provided this conforms to love, participate in any sacrifice that resistance asks of you to overcome our present travail. (KP 5.3, original emphasis)

These frequent quotes and references to various parts of the Bible give witness to the religious and Christian character of the kairos documents individually and kairos theology as a whole.[3] They provide context and an interpretative lens for both the social analysis and the political recommendations and moral actions suggested. It is particularly noteworthy how this biblical language is not limited to dedicated theological paragraphs or a few selected topics. It appears throughout these documents as an integrated dimension of its form and contents and becomes a key feature of the language of kairos theology.

---

3. For more on the use of sacred texts and the Bible in the public sphere, see Kim and Draper, *Liberating Texts* and Kittredge, Aitken, and Draper, *Bible in the Public Square*.

Language and Voice

THE WORD OF GOD

The many biblical references make it necessary for the kairos documents to address the issue of biblical interpretation. In the South African kairos document the need for valid and contextual Bible interpretations is emphasized and seen as the missing dimension of certain forms of theology: "What has been overlooked here is one of the most fundamental of all principles of biblical interpretation: every text must be interpreted *in its context*" (KSA 2.1, original emphasis). While literal Bible reading is rejected, emphasis is put on contextual hermeneutics.

The same is the case in the *The Road to Damascus*. In its discussion of the faith of the poor and in retelling the history of colonialization and European mission, they explain how a movement of resistance emerged. This also implied a new way of reading the scriptures:

> The Christians who were part of this development began to read the Bible with new eyes. We were no longer dependent upon the interpretations of our oppressors.
>
> What we discovered was that Jesus was one of us. He was born in poverty. He did not become incarnate as a king or nobleman but as one of the poor and oppressed. He took sides with the poor, supported their cause and blessed them. On the other hand, he condemned the rich. "Blessed are you who are poor" *(Lk 6:20)* "Woe to you who are rich" *(Lk 6:24)*. He even described his mission as the liberation of the downtrodden *(Lk 4:18)*. That was the very opposite of what we had been taught.
>
> At the heart of Jesus' message was the coming of the Reign of God. We discovered that Jesus had promised the Reign of God to the poor: "Yours is the Reign of God" *(Lk 6:20)* and that the good news about the coming of God's Reign was supposed to be good news for the poor *(Lk 4:18)*. (RD 35-37, original emphasis)

This reign of God leads in turn to a discussion of the image of God and the understanding of Jesus. The kairos authors write:

> Jesus was and still is the Word of God, the true image of God. (...) The God we see in the face of Jesus is the God who hears the cries of the poor and who leads them across the sea and the desert to the promised land *(Ex 3:17)*. The true God is the God of the poor who is angry about injustice in the world, vindicates the poor *(Ps 103:6)*, pulls down the mighty from their thrones and lifts up the lowly *(Lk 1:52)*. This is the God who will judge all human beings according to what they have done or not done for the hungry, the

thirsty, the naked, the sick and those in prison *(Mt 25:31–46)*. (RD 40, original emphasis)

In *Kairos Palestine* the assessment of theological propositions takes place in the form of a reflection on how the Word of God should be understood and biblical texts read. Jesus is referred to as "God's eternal Word" (KP 2.1.1) and the Word of God understood as "a living Word, casting a particular light on each period of history" (KP 2.2.2). Rather than formulating a hermeneutical principle, the authors present three different biblical quotes (Heb 1:1–2; Lk 24:27 and Mk 1:27) seemingly making the Protestant idea of the Scripture as its own interpreter, the implicit principle for Bible interpretation.

Given that "God has spoken to humanity" (KP 2.2) a universal perspective is emphasized. The authors of *Kairos Palestine* proclaim their belief in "one God, Creator of the universe and of humanity [and] a good and just God, who loves each one of his creatures" (KP 2.1). This is a creed that can unite Christians of different denominations, and indicates both the universal and the normative orientation in the document. This universal outlook also implies an inclusive approach to peoples of other faiths, and more specifically is kept in a tone recognizable and in line with Jewish and Muslim beliefs. In this way, the particular Christian perspective in *Kairos Palestine* is combined with an emphasis on humanity, universality, and inclusiveness.

This universal outlook and understanding of the Word of God is articulated with reference to several specifically Christian teachings. This is done through a reference to Heb 1:1–2 and how "*God has spoken to us by a Son*" (KP 2.2, original emphasis), that "Jesus Christ came in order to fulfil the Law and the Prophets" (KP 2.2.1), and that he came with "*a new teaching*" (Mk 1:27)" (KP 2.2.2, original emphasis). The understanding of the Word of God is explained in more detail as "a living Word (. . .) manifesting to Christian believers what God is saying to us here and now. For this reason, it is unacceptable to transform the Word of God into letters of stone" (KP 2.2.2). Accordingly, there seems to be an implied notion of the Word of God as something dynamic, manifesting itself always in the particular.

Thus, a close connection between contemporary Bible reading and social analysis, politics, and ethics is established in kairos theology. Bible reading provides perspectives on the current situation, while the Word of God is both "eternal" and a "living Word." As a result, the authors explicitly

Language and Voice

distance themselves from what is described as a "fundamentalist Biblical interpretation that brings us death and destruction" (KP 2.2.2).

THEOLOGICAL TERMINOLOGY

The religious language in the kairos documents is not limited to references to, and quotes from, biblical passages. The use of theologically charged terms to describe and analyze social conditions is a kairos theology trademark. One example of this theological terminology is the concept of *evil*. In the South African document it is pointed out how the state theology has its "symbol of evil" (KSA 2.3) and the Palestinian document refers to oppression and suffering as "the evil" (KP 4.2.5). The latter document also highlights the necessity of not "accepting evil or aggression" but "to correct the evil and stop the aggression" (KP 4.2.1). *Kairos Palestine* argues there is a "duty to liberate [our country] from the evil of injustice and war" (KP 2.3.1) and that "[h]ope means not giving in to evil" (KP 3.2). People are encouraged "to vanquish the evil of war" (KP 3.5). The authors refer to the Israeli occupation of Palestine as "an evil and a sin that must be resisted and removed" (KP 4.2.1).

The term *idolatry* is another theologically laden concept that appears in kairos theology and in particular in *The Road to Damascus*. Idolatry is here understood as "the sin of worshipping or being subservient to someone or something which is not God" (RD 49). To denote actual attitudes and practices as idolatry is described as a key dimension of the prophetic call. The authors argue idolatry "is not simply an inability to see and hear; it is a refusal to see and hear. It is not merely lack of faith in the God of life; it is the worship of a false god" (RD 46). As idolatry leads Christians to other sins—"heresy and apostasy, hypocrisy and blasphemy" (RD 48)—it is seen as a prime cause for the present crisis. Thus, sin does not have here, as in *Kairos South Africa*, a specific reference to a political regime or tyranny, but rather "a system in which consumerist materialism has been enthroned as a god" (RD 50). Further, *The Road to Damascus* argues idols "rule by fear and intimidation or by trying to buy people, to bribe them and seduce them with money" (RD 51). The idol "*demands absolute submission and blind obedience*" (RD 51, original emphasis), and represents the "*denial of all hope for the future*" (RD 52, original emphasis). Thus, *The Road to Damascus* links sin, idolatry, and blasphemy:

> Idolatry is a sin against the first commandment. Of all the sins related to it, none is more scandalous than the sin against the second commandment—blasphemy. "You shall not utter the name of Yahweh your God to misuse it" *(Ex 20:7)*. It is blasphemy to misuse the name of God in defense of imperialism. (. . .) To invoke the name of the God of life to justify death and destruction is blasphemy. It is giving scandal to the little ones *(Mk 9:42; Lk 17:1-2)*. (RD 80)

As with the biblical language, this kind of theological terminology is explicit throughout the kairos documents. It is closely linked to the biblical language, but expands and explains this to the reader in the same way that this terminology provides kairos theology with unique interpretative resources as it seeks to analyze and understand "what is happening" and the challenges people face in times of crisis.

THE HOLY LAND

The discussion of land in *Kairos Palestine* is particularly instructive in regard to the issue of language and voice in kairos theology. The role of land in Christian theology and the Israeli-Palestinian political discourse is a key issue in this document.

In Christian theology God is the Creator of the universe and all human beings, but Jesus is seen as the incarnation of this God in history. Several of the biblical narratives take place in the geographical area widely referred to today as Israel and Palestine: in Judea, Jerusalem, Bethlehem etc. The interpretation and importance of land and specific, geographical places vary within Christianity and between Christian individuals, groups, and churches. Considering that the Old Testament includes several notions of land[4] and how the New Testament only expands the interpretative space available, this is not surprising. This plurality of positions prepares, however, the ground for conflicting interpretations and heated debate.[5]

Kairos Palestine deals primarily with the dispossession and military occupation of Palestinian land. Accordingly, *the land* is a territorial concept that refers to a specific geographical area called Palestine. This is the document's national and political interpretation of the concept of the land.

---

4. See Brueggemann, *The Land* and Habel, *The Land Is Mine*.

5. For more on the issue of the land, see Davies, *Gospel and the Land*; Chapman, *Whose Promised Land?*; Burge, *Whose Land?*; March, *God's Land on Loan*; Burge, *Jesus and the Land*; and Katanacho, *Land of Christ*.

Language and Voice

The authors see themselves as representing both "Christian and Muslim Palestinians" (KP 2.3.2), and the common plight and suffering of Christian and Muslim Palestinians is emphasized: "We suffer from the occupation of our land because we are Palestinians" (KP 2.3.4). In line with the concern for "all the inhabitants of this land" (KP Introduction), an inclusive and non-ethnic understanding of the land is presented. This is articulated through the theological notion that the land belongs to God. The authors explain that:

> Our land is God's land, as is the case with all countries in the world. It is holy in as much as God is present in it, for God alone is holy and sanctifier. It is the duty of those of us who live here, to respect the will of God for this land. It is our duty to liberate it from the evil of injustice and war. It is God's land and therefore it must be a land of reconciliation, peace and love. (KP 2.3.1)

This understanding of Palestine as God's land is, in contrast to the national and political interpretation of the concept of the land, a religious or theological interpretation of the land that understands the land along the inclusive, non-ethnic, and universal lines already noted. Palestine does not belong exclusively to Palestinians, nor to Christians or Muslims, but to the Creator of all human beings.

Thus, when discussing the religious significance of Israel and Palestine in Judaism, Christianity, and Islam, the universal outlook in the document is highlighted. The authors emphasize that "our land has a universal mission" (KP 2.3), and see the Promised land as part of God's plan for universal salvation. At the same time the uniqueness of "our country" is downplayed. Through this universal interpretation the conflict potential in the theologies of the biblical land promises are significantly downplayed. The document explicitly rejects an understanding of the Promised land as a political program and argues "[i]n light of the teachings of the Holy Bible, the promise of the land has never been a political program, but rather the prelude to complete universal salvation. It was the initiation of the fulfilment of the Kingdom of God on earth" (KP 2.3).

In other words, in *Kairos Palestine* the notion of a promised, Holy Land is interpreted as a universal mission and hope for all, rather than a particular or political promise for some. This is followed by the accentuation of the connectedness of "Christian and Muslim Palestinians" (KP 2.3.2), a connectedness which is also described as a "natural right" (KP 2.3.4). This leads the authors to reject "any use of the Bible to legitimize or support political options or positions that are based upon injustice" (KP 2.4) and to "declare that the Israeli occupation of Palestinian land is a sin against God and humanity because it deprives the Palestinians of their basic human rights, bestowed by God" (KP 2.5). The authors argue that "God created us not so that we might engage in strife and conflict but rather that we might come and know and love one another, and together build up the land in love and mutual respect" (KP 2.1).

This notion of the universal mission becomes a key concept in both the document's general theological outlook and its understanding of the land in particular. The universal understanding of the concept of the land does not rely, however, exclusively on this notion of God as the Creator of everyone and everything. The role and meaning of the land is also interpreted in light of the Gospel of Jesus and thus has particular Christian characteristics. The authors argue that:

> Our Lord Jesus Christ came, proclaiming that the Kingdom of God was near. He provoked a revolution in the life and faith of all humanity. He came with *"a new teaching"* (Mk 1:27), casting a new light on the Old Testament, on the themes that relate to our Christian faith and our daily lives, themes such as the promises, the election, the people of God and the land. (KP 2.2.2, original emphasis)

The contrast thus established between the Old Testament on the one hand and the Gospel proclaimed by Jesus on the other hand, prepares the ground for a Christological perspective that is seen to cast new light on the Christian faith and tradition, biblical texts, and the lives of Christian Palestinians. This does not lead, however, to a revision of the universal emphasis derived from the notion of God as Creator. On the contrary, this emphasis is maintained in the Christological perspective, given how Jesus proclaimed and "provoked a revolution in the life and faith of all of humanity." Accordingly, the Christological interpretation of the land becomes just another source for the universal outlook and interpretation of the land emphasized in the document.

One important implication of this theologically informed interpretation of the land is that the narrative of both Israel and Palestine is rewritten in a visionary and prophetic manner. The authors offer a new vision of a land for everyone and a "land of reconciliation, peace and love," in stark contrast to the political realities of the day. Still, this prophetic vision relates to the contemporary political discourse and the political interpretation of the land by suggesting an alternative way of envisioning the political future in Israel and Palestine.

TRANSLATION AND BILINGUALISM

An important concern in public theology is that it should not only be intelligible and persuasive to Christians and church members, but also to the plurality of different audiences in the public sphere. As noted above, there are those who for such reasons argue these contributions should rely on a widely shared secular language. Others, for example Nicholas Wolterstorff, argue every citizen should "use whatever reasons they find appropriate— including, then, religious reasons."[6] Some go further and say that not only can religious language be used, but that it should be used. As Jeffrey Stout puts it in *Ethics after Babel*:

> Serious conversation with theology will be greatly limited if the voice of theology is not recognizably theological. Conversation partners must remain distinctive enough to be identified, to be needed. They must be able to clarify the difference their outlook makes and to say why they differ from the rest of us at the most crucial points.[7]

Similarly, Benne draws on Michal Perry's concept of "ecumenical political dialogue" and agrees with Perry that the church should draw explicitly on its specifically religious symbols, values, and language. Indeed, he suggests that "religious arguments flowing from core religious and moral convictions will be healthily challenged and enriched by "robust external deliberation.""[8] This is backed up by three additional arguments: firstly, that they are not necessarily unintelligible and secondly, that a public argument shorn of its religious assumptions is "finally and radically incomplete without such beliefs."[9] Thirdly, it is argued that substantive contributions are needed in the public debate:

> In a political world dominated by interest group liberalism, where the adjudication of claims is attempted purely on procedural grounds, substantive moral traditions are increasingly necessary

---

6. Audi and Wolterstorff, *Religion in the Public Square*, 112.
7. Stout, *Ethics after Babel*, 184. See also Stout, *Democracy and Tradition*.
8. Benne, *Paradoxical Vision*, 213.
9. Ibid.

INTERRUPTION AND IMAGINATION

for the health of public discourse itself. A public square denuded of substantive moral proposals will likely revert to struggles of private power rather than public persuasion, thus decreasing the chance for peaceful accommodation of competing claims.[10]

These debates about the very character of doing sound public theology point to the problem of language and voice in public theology. A commonly held position among scholars in the field is that bilingualism is possible. They acknowledge that while Christian faith has its own language and idiom, the language in the public sphere needs to be a secular language with limited references to the transcendent, religious, or spiritual. They maintain, however, that it is possible to translate the Christian faith and message into the secular language of the public sphere, and thus give a theological contribution to this context. Accordingly, public theology operates with two languages: the religious, Christian language on the one hand, and the modern, secular language on the other hand. As Bedford-Strom puts it: "the public theological notion of bilinguality honours the fact that, in a pluralistic society, the public existence of the church requires a self-reflective effort to make ethical insights gained from Christian traditions plausible for all people of good will."[11]

Graham links this to the interdisciplinary and dialogical nature of public theology. She argues:

> Public theology speaks of itself as 'bilingual' in drawing from the resources of its own tradition while listening to, and being comprehensible by, non-theological disciplines. This is only right if it is not only to address the interests of the Church but the well-being of the world. The aim is engagement, and public theology tries to practices what it preaches in conducting its researches dialogically and *in public*, through colloquia, consultation and dialogue with policy-makers and activists.[12]

This premise in public theology has been criticized and rejected, not least from a post-liberal position and from the perspective of radical orthodoxy. Hauerwas has insisted that the church must "be church" in its public witness[13] and has argued that a kind of translation of the Christian language into secular language implies losing the Christian identity and character of

---

10. Ibid., 214.
11. Bedford-Strohm, "Public Theology and Political Ethics," 287.
12. Graham, *Between a Rock and a Hard Place*, 99–100, original emphasis.
13. Hauerwas, *Truthfulness and Tragedy* and Hauerwas, *In Good Company*.

this witness.[14] For Hauerwas, the bilingualism defended in public theology does not hold. Indeed, bilingualism risks being a naive exercise in translation, assuming that every translation is straight forward and disregarding the obvious risks of being lost in translation.

One response to this criticism is to argue that public theology needs to be more creative. Pointing out the limitations of universal Esperanto, Stout argues religious (and also secular) people should develop a so-called bricolage, i.e., they should construct positions by borrowing from the variety of moral fragments that exist in modern-postmodern societies.[15] Besides borrowing, bricoleurs jostle and negotiate. Practitioners of public theology can also use so-called pidgin-language, i.e., a language like human rights language that is accessible to a variety of religious and secular traditions. The use of this language by such a variety of people enriches and thickens this language, so that it eventually develops into a creole language. As Koopman points out: "This *creole* language remains accessible to people from various traditions, but it is thicker and more tradition-dependent than the pidgin."[16]

With the frequent biblical quotes and references, as well as theological terminology, the kairos documents present themselves with a distinct religious voice and combining this with a secular language. In this way, kairos theology contrast with approaches that reject the validity or legitimacy of religious language in the public sphere. The kairos documents are, however, not only bilingual, but multilingual. They combine languages and let them interpret each other by joining fragments in different ways and thus developing a creative pidgin or creole language of faith and social commitment.

DIFFERENT DISCOURSES

The way kairos theology speaks in different languages at the same time, creatively combining and enriching them, highlights how public theology can express itself in different ways, not only with different languages but also in a variety of voices, theological moods or moral discourses.

David Ford distinguishes between five different theological moods that all belong to the theological discourse.[17] Firstly, theology must give

14. Hauerwas, "On Keeping Theological Ethics," 30.
15. Stout, *Ethics after Babel*, 77–81.
16. Koopman, "Churches and Public Policy," 46, original emphasis.
17. Ford, *Future of Christian Theology*, 68–83.

testimony and tell the story of Christian hope and promise. This is the indicative and narrative theological mood. Secondly, theology must share the imperatives of the law and Christian teaching. Thirdly, theology must ask questions based on the interrogative prophecy and lament found in the Bible. This is the interrogative mood of theological discourse. Fourthly, theology has a subjunctive mood that is expressed through wisdom and parables, and, fifthly, there is an optative mood characterized by praise and apocalyptic vision.

More concerned about Christian theology in relation to ethical issues, politics, and public policy, James M. Gustafson distinguishes between prophetic, narrative, ethical, and policy discourses. Prophetic discourse addresses "the *root* of religious, moral, or social waywardness, not specific instances in which certain policies are judged to be inadequate or wrong."[18] In addition it has an utopian aspect and is used to "proclaim and depict an ideal state of affairs which is radically in contrast with the actual state of affairs in which we live together in society."[19]

Narrative discourse has three interrelated functions. They "sustain and confirm the religious and moral identity of the Christian community, and evoke and sustain the faithfulness of its members to Jesus Christ,"[20] but also appeal to empathy and emotions. Thirdly, it "evokes the imagination, stimulates our moral sensibilities and affections [and] enlarges one's vision of what is going on."[21]

Ethical discourse comes in the form of "philosophical modes of argument and analysis,"[22] and Gustafson argues that "every serious Christian group that makes moral proposals for the wider public must at least acknowledge and come to grips with this issue: the relation of Christian particularity to the universal in morality."[23]

Finally, policy discourse seeks to "recommend or prescribe quite particular courses of action about quite specific issues."[24] This discourse is articulated "not by external observers, but by the persons who have a responsibility to make choices and to carry out the actions that are required

---

18. Gustafson, "Varieties of Moral Discourse," 50, original emphasis.
19. Ibid., 53.
20. Ibid., 56.
21. Ibid., 57.
22. Ibid., 63.
23. Ibid., 65–66.
24. Ibid., 71.

by the choices."²⁵ It is also a discourse particularly concerned with the conditions that limit and enable policy making and implementation.

As all of these have shortcomings, Gustafson argues none of these varieties of moral discourse are sufficient in themselves. Prophetic discourse "involves a necessary simplification of what are, from other perspectives, very complex problems and issues. (. . .) It does not concern itself with incremental choices that have to be made by persons and institutions in which good and evil are intricately intermingled."²⁶ Narrative ethics needs to be "checked against more rational analysis," and is, as prophetic discourse, of limited use when dealing with particular issues and political choices.²⁷ While ethical discourse does not have the capacity to identify evil or the ability to "move persons with a sense of urgency"²⁸ the policy discourse needs to have "their arguments and choices clarified, evaluated, and informed by the ethician."²⁹

Lisa Sowle Cahill has supplemented Gustafson's four varieties with a fifth: participatory discourse. This is:

> a mode of theological and ethical speech in which its practical roots and outcomes are intentionally acknowledged" and that has a "power to allude to or induce a shared sphere of behavior, oriented by shared concerns and goals, and (. . .) to constitute relations of empathy and interdependence.³⁰

While Gustafson's four varieties are verbal, the participatory discourse is action or practice oriented. This too, however, should not stand on its own and needs to be informed by the other modes of discourse. Koopman uses these all of these varieties of moral discourse to describe what he calls the prophetic task of the church. In addition to the traditional prophetic roles of:

> firstly, the envisioning of a new society and secondly, the criticism of the imperfect status quo, prophetic speaking is extended, thirdly, to include the role of story-telling, i.e., the telling of stories of suffering and despair, as well as victory and hope of people. Prophetic speaking fourthly entails participating in technical philosophical

25. Ibid., 71–72.
26. Ibid., 55.
27. Ibid., 60.
28. Ibid., 70.
29. Ibid., 75.
30. Cahill, *Theological Bioethics*, 38.

discourses in which concepts are roughly defined, illuminating distinctions and nuances are offered, and well-argued decisions are made. Lastly, participation in policy discourses is described as a crucial form of prophetic speaking.[31]

In the kairos documents several, if not all, of these are represented. There is Christian witness, stories of suffering, and narratives of hope. There is lament and a moral call to work for justice and peace. The authors put forward challenging questions, suggest answers and praise God as they trust He or She will deliver them from evil. Similarly, there is a prophetic call for radical change, an appeal to empathy and emotions, but also an ethical analysis of right and wrong in a given situation. Last but not least, specific policy measures are outlined to deal with this situation. This multitude of voices, moods, or discourses is a key characteristic of kairos theology and the appeal and convincing power of the kairos documents seems closely related to this creative pluralism of language and voice.

LANGUAGE AND VOICE IN TIMES OF CRISIS

The language of public theology needs to consider and communicate across the divide between the Christian community, narratives, and particular traditions on the one hand, and the pluralistic, postmodern, and post-secular wider society on the other. Turning to, and using, the assumed widely accessible secular language is one option, but not without costs. This language blurs the unique and specific flavor of Christian witness and in some cases particular religious concerns seem difficult to translate into a universal language, which indicates how translation is not an innocent activity. Public theology can come across as speaking to different languages and giving different messages to different audiences. In the attempt to please its audience public theology risks losing authenticity, credibility, and its recognizable character.

The kairos documents point towards a more constructive alternative: unashamed biblical and theological language used to address all kinds of audiences, but always combined with a variety of languages and discourses available to Church, society, and thus public theology. The religious language resonates with narratives of other "comprehensive doctrines," religions, and world views. The Bible references also seem to supplement and

---

31. Koopman, "Churches and Public Policy Discourses," 41–42.

strengthen the social analysis and to lend theological legitimacy to the authors' interpretations and moral recommendations. Further, by using theological concepts to describe and analyze society, a theological interpretation is given. In this way, characteristics of contemporary social life are inserted into an interpretive frame: biblical material and the Christian tradition.

This way of dealing with the problem of language and voice in public theology has both problems and prospects. By utilizing this form of theological terminology to conceptualize for example Israel's (evil) occupation and the situation in Palestine, some find the kairos authors demonize their opponents. The sharp language used can be in contrast to the otherwise reconciling tone of the document. In this way, the voice of the kairos theology can come across as harsh and conflictual, although there is a message of shared interests, common good and hope for future reconciliation in all of them. The use of religious language and theological terminology also seems to rely on a certain degree of religious literacy on the part of the recipient or audience. In addition, the use of different discourses might come across as multiple messages.

On the other hand, kairos theology suggests an immensely creative and imaginative way of doing public theology. The documents combine the particular and the universal, the religious and the secular in a fluent manner, letting one be informed and interpreted by the other. The use of religious language and theological terminology, including religious narratives, provide the documents with their unique voice and character and thus enables a unique contribution to the public sphere.

Even in times of crisis public theology needs to retain its combination of rational, secular language on the one hand, and the theological, religious language on the other hand. Combining them implies not letting one replace the other, but that the two inform each other. In this way, the secular citizen is invited to listen, but also to explore and learn from the realm of religious language and perspectives. The religious language provides an alternative interpretation of the crisis at hand, and, significantly, is a resource that can be used to highlight the moral and existential aspects of a given crisis.

8

The Climate Crisis

As theological resources, perspectives, and insights are expressed and made relevant in the public sphere, public theology is redefined and reinterpreted. The kairos documents represent a constructive contribution to this on-going reinterpretation of both the practice and study of public theology. In the preceding chapters I have used three of them as a platform for discussing key features and problems of public theology in times of crisis.

These kairos documents are statements issued in response to particular crises and contextual challenges in South Africa, the global South, and Palestine. They are all, however, motivated and informed by a Christian outlook and they follow the same structure: they provide a social analysis, give a theological interpretation of the crisis at hand, and call for actions and policy measures to be taken. In this way, these documents are examples of an interdisciplinary merger of theology, social, and ethical analysis and it is in the interaction between these that a critical, creative, and constructive contribution to the public sphere emerges and suggests a model for public theology.

Today the global community is faced with yet another crisis: unprecedented climate change resulting in storms, floods, famine etc. Churches and Christians in local communities across the world are affected in different ways and again turn to the sources of their faith looking for resources to interpret and respond to the challenges of the day. Indeed, contemporary climate change can be described as our kairos. As the Ecumenical Patriarch Bartholomew has pointed out:

> As individuals we are often conscious of a kairos, a moment when we make a choice that will affect our whole lives. For the human race as whole, there is now a kairos, a decisive time in our relationship with God's creation. We will either act in time to protect life on earth from the worst consequences of human folly, or we will fail to act.[1]

This is a challenge to all of us—as individuals, concerned citizens, civil society, and governments—and it is an acute challenge. Action needs to be taken now and public theology must offer policy relevant advice and moral guidance. However, several questions remain: How should public theology understand this crisis? Which actions should public theology recommend and how should public theology address these issues?[2]

In this chapter I will not put forward a comprehensive Christian ecotheology, but briefly outline how a kairos inspired public theology might respond to these issues. First I look at how the international community, religious actors, and academics have addressed the ecological crisis and climate change. I then present different theological responses to these issues and Bedford-Strohm's five guidelines for a public theology of ecology. Against this background, I outline how a kairos inspired public theology might address the climate crisis.

THE ENVIRONMENT AND CLIMATE CHANGE

Environmental issues and climate change have been on the international agenda for decades. Publications by Rachel Carson, the Club of Rome, and others in the 1960s contributed, however, to an increased awareness of the threats to modern culture and a critique of Western lifestyle.[3] This made people all the more aware of the consequences of industrialization and mass-consumption and the impact this had on the ecological balance and the wider environment.

The international community responded already in the early 1970s. In 1972 the UN organized its first Conference on the Human Environment (UNCHE) and established the United Nations Environment Program (UNEP). Since then a series of UN conferences and initiatives have

---

1. Quoted in Rossing, "God Laments with Us," 126.

2. For more on the discussions about climate change, see Hulme, *Why We Disagree* and Giddens, *Politics of Climate Change*.

3. Carson, *Silent Spring* and Meadows and Club of Rome, *Limits to Growth*.

followed, including the World Commission on Environment and Development which submitted its report *Our Common Future* in 1987.[4] The United Nations Conference on Environment and Development in Rio 1992 resulted in an action plan for sustainable development in the new millennium known as Agenda 21. The same meeting also produced the United Nations Framework Convention on Climate Change (UNFCCC), an international treaty to limit global temperature increases. Since this came into force in 1994 a series of Conferences of the Parties have taken place (COP-meetings). The third of these, in 1997, adopted the Kyoto Protocol which legally binds developed countries to reduce their emissions. Later meetings have negotiated and renegotiated the Kyoto Protocol, but have consistently struggled to reach international consensus. The Paris agreement in 2015 was by some considered a historic, ambitious plan, while others criticized it for lacking firm commitments and binding enforcement mechanisms.

The academic community has also taken on the challenge of understanding and responding to climate change. Within both the natural and the social sciences climate change has received increased attention over the years. The Intergovernmental Panel on Climate Change (IPCC), established under the auspices of the United Nations (UN) by the United Nations Environment Program (UNEP) and the World Meteorological Organization (WMO) in 1988, "reviews and assesses the most recent scientific, technical and socio-economic information produced worldwide relevant to the understanding of climate change."[5] Neither has climate change gone by unnoticed by scholars in fields such as the humanities, religious studies, philosophy, theology, and ethics.[6]

Various religious actors have also seen themselves challenged by environmental issues and climate change and sought to find ways to respond adequately. A series of climate state statements have been issued both from the different faith communities individually and in the form of interreligious cooperation.[7] The engagement of the Council for the World Parliaments of Religions (CPWR) on climate change, the Interfaith Declaration on Climate Change (IDCC), and the World and the Interfaith Summit on

---

4. Brundtland, "Our Common Future."

5. http://www.ipcc.ch/organization/organization.shtml.

6. Lodge and Hamlin, *Religion and the New Ecology* and Tanner and Mitchell, *Religion and the Environment*.

7. A number of climate change statements from world religions can be found on the website for the Forum on Religion and Ecology at Yale: http://fore.research.yale.edu/climate-change/statements-from-world-religions/.

The Climate Crisis

Climate Change in New York in 2014 are all expressions of religious actors coming together to give their joint contribution to halt climate change. Within the Christian tradition, the World Council of Churches' (WCC) program for *Justice, Peace and Integrity of Creation* (JPIC) launched in 1983 has been an especially important contribution. Similarly the Lutheran World Federation (LWF) has addressed climate change, as have the umbrella organizations of other denominations and a large number of national and regional churches.

This involvement of religious actors in these issues has only grown over the years, and they are increasingly recognized as an important voice in the global and political discussions on international climate change and justice. Three statements can exemplify and illustrate how various religious actors have expressed themselves: The Interfaith Summit on Climate Change (2014), the Swedish Lutheran Bishops (2014), and Pope Francis (2015).

The Interfaith Summit on Climate Change in New York in 2014 stated:

> As representatives from different faith and religious traditions, we stand together to express deep concern for the consequences of climate change on the earth and its people, all entrusted, as our faiths reveal, to our common care. Climate change is indeed a threat to life, a precious gift we have received and that we need to care for.[8]

Secondly, Swedish bishops have issued *A Bishops' Letter about the Climate*, arguing that:

> Existence has always seemed almost limitless. There was a new continent to colonies when Europe became too poor and densely populated. Easily accessible energy has been available for a few hundred years. It has been so cheap that we have been able to squander it. We have quite simply become used to being able to expand out of crises. We have now reached a few limits. More greenhouse gases in the atmosphere will definitely destabilize the climate. Will the earth be able to provide food for all of its billions of human inhabitants? Is fair distribution feasible when the struggle for survival becomes tougher? Does peace have any chance? Has God equipped us to meet this crisis too? Do we have the spiritual, mental and material resources to meet this challenge? Can the basic structure of giving that Christian faith anticipates in

---

8. http://interfaithclimate.org/the-statement/.

life make us release our tight grip on what we have achieved and see the opportunities for and joy in a changed lifestyle?[9]

Thirdly, Pope Francis opens his statement on climate change with these words:

> "LAUDATO SI', mi' Signore"—"Praise be to you, my Lord." In the words of this beautiful canticle, Saint Francis of Assisi reminds us that our common home is like a sister with whom we share our life and a beautiful mother who opens her arms to embrace us. "Praise be to you, my Lord, through our Sister, Mother Earth, who sustains and governs us, and who produces various fruit with colored flowers and herbs."[10]

All of these are examples of public theology put into practice. Their full versions include more social analysis and reflections on the political and ethical imperatives of our time, but already in these fragments the religious flavor of the language and voice of these statements is evident.

PUBLIC THEOLOGY, ECOLOGY, AND CLIMATE CHANGE

As concerns for the non-human creation—animals, plants, and the earth—can be found both in the Bible and in the Christian tradition, these statements are not surprising. In fact, contemporary Christian engagement with such issues appeared in parallel with the growing environmental concern in the Western world in the 1960s. In response to this increased awareness several different theologies have emerged in response to the ecological crisis and climate change.[11] Some theologians have focused on how the relationship between God, human beings, and the non-human creation is perceived[12] and constructively suggested forms of eco-theology.[13] Others

---

9. Church of Sweden, "A Bishops' Letter."

10. Quoting Francis, of Assisi, "Canticle of the Creatures," 1:113–14; see http://w2.vatican.va/content/francesco/en/encyclicals/documents/papa-francesco_20150524_enciclica-laudato-si.html.

11. Bedford-Strohm and Deane-Drummond, *Religion and Ecology* and Jenkins, *Future of Ethics*.

12. Cobb, *Is It Too Late?* and Santmire, *Travail of Nature*.

13. Deane-Drummond, *Eco-Theology* and Habel and Trudinger, *Exploring Ecological Hermeneutics*.

have developed a theological and ethical cultural critique of modern consumerist societies.[14]

Public theologian Sebastian Kim has identified four such strands of theologies: social ecology, creation theology, eco-feminism, and eco-spirituality.[15] The first of these, social ecology, argues that nature or creation suffers under the bondage and injustice of socio-political structures and therefore is in need of liberation. It becomes the responsibility of humankind to assist in the struggle to achieve justice for the whole of creation. Creation theology argues that creation must be seen in relation to God. This approach thus rejects the anthropocentrism of traditional Christian theology and argues that human beings are not set apart from creation, but part of, and dependent on, nature. Rather than separation and domination, the key words here are interconnectedness and interdependence.

Eco-feminism shares with social ecology an emphasis on oppression and exploitation, but draws on feminist theology and primal and indigenous religions rather than liberation theology. This leads eco-feminism to reject any dualism between God and creation. Finally, eco-spirituality also draws on resources from primal religions, but here a stronger emphasis is put on the Holy Spirit. The interconnectedness between humankind and nature is emphasized, resulting in a biocentric and holistic world view.

Addressing more explicitly the interpretation and political implications of the crisis at hand, Bedford-Strohm has developed what he calls five guidelines for a public theology of ecology.[16] Firstly, he argues, a public theology of ecology must reclaim its own traditions. This is not, however, simply a matter of transplanting biblical statements into the policy discourse. Barbara Rossing is obviously right when stating: "There is no direct link between the Bible and climate change. We must be clear on this point. The Bible does not "predict" this crisis as punishment for sinners, contrary to what some fundamentalists claim. I do think, however, that we can draw on the Bible to speak to this crisis."[17] Bedford-Strohm acknowledges this need for interpretation, but argues that biblical texts affirm "the independent dignity of a non-human creation equally created by God."[18]

---

14. Northcott, *Moral Climate* and McFague, *Blessed Are the Consumers*.
15. Kim, *Theology in the Public Sphere*, 57–76.
16. Bedford-Strohm, "Public Theology of Ecology and Civil Society."
17. Rossing, "God Laments with Us," 120.
18. Bedford-Strohm, "Public Theology of Ecology and Civil Society," 50.

Secondly, Bedford-Strohm argues public theology of ecology should acknowledge the conflict between human beings and non-human nature and thus reject a naive and romantic understanding of nature. Thirdly, as political decision making implies dealing with dilemmas these must be acknowledged. Fourthly, it is necessary to critically reflect on fundamental socio-cultural values and to reorient social values. Finally, Bedford-Strohm argues public theology should provide ethical and realistic guidance for such political decision making.

KAIROS THEOLOGY AND CLIMATE CHANGE

A public theology inspired by kairos theology would agree with Bedford-Strohm on the need to reclaim Christianity's own tradition. Indeed, public theology should not only reclaim the Christian tradition, biblical language and theological terminology, but use this in an integrated and innovative manner to illuminate and interpret the crisis we all are facing. A public theology of this kind could speak about God's creation (Gen 1–2) and how "all creation is still groaning and is in pain" (Rom 8:22). It would be biblically grounded and theologically rooted in the Word of God and the Christian tradition, but also make use of the wide range of theological moods and moral discourses this tradition offers.

Similarly, a public theology inspired by kairos theology would agree that the conflict between human beings and non-human nature should be acknowledged, as should the dilemmas involved in political decision making. However, this kind of public theology would also emphasize the conflicts that shape the debates on climate change in the public sphere and in political decision making and not least highlight the living conditions of men, women, and children and those who carry the burdens of this crisis. These are the poor, oppressed, and marginalized in society and those who feel the impact of floods, drought, and hurricanes more than others. A public theology inspired by the kairos documents would speak out about these inequalities and injustices and thus interrupt the day-to-day dealings of politics, policy making, and public debate with a positioned analysis and normative conclusions. In this way it would, again in agreement with Bedford-Strohm, reflect on and challenge the sociocultural values of contemporary culture. Indeed, this kind of public theology would identify the irreconcilable conflicts of contemporary society, challenge dominant discourses and implicit understandings. It would suggest compromise where possible, but reject neutrality towards injustice and compromise without justice.

In terms of ethical and realistic guidance for political decision making, a public theology inspired by kairos theology would also spell out the practical implications of its social analysis. In the case of climate change, public theology could call for divestment from coal, strong limits on oil production, and an end to fracking. In other words, it would call for a green economy. These recommendations would not be utopian and beyond any conceivable practical solution to address the issue, but would seek to stretch the imagination of what might be realistically possible.

Acknowledging the conflicts and dilemmas involved in such policy making, as well as the historical and tentative character of its analysis and judgement, these practical implications and recommendations would be presented as context-dependent suggestions and proposals. This is not to say that they are only proposals, but by being the result of a considered socio-political and theological assessment, they shed light on this analysis and point towards possible policy implications. In this way, a kairos inspired public theology could interrupt the current discursive patterns of on-going climate debates and be a resource to expand the imagination of the public sphere.

PUBLIC THEOLOGY IN TIMES OF CLIMATE CRISIS

There is both continuity and discontinuity between the examples of public theology presented here and the various forms of eco-theology developed in recent decades on the one hand, and kairos theology on the other hand. To sum up, I will now highlight some of the key characteristics of a kairos inspired public theology in relation to climate change.

Firstly, a kairotic public theology would offer a comprehensive empirical, critical, and normative social analysis of the climate crisis. The analysis would be empirically focused of what is happening on the ground in local communities where people live their lives and rooted in the experiences of the poor and marginalized. From this perspective it would seek to uncover the consequences of climate change in terms of suffering and injustice, and thus to challenge the status quo.

Secondly, a public theology inspired by kairos theology would in this sense keep its primary loyalty with the poor, oppressed, and suffering. It would, however, not only rely on the experiences, interpretations, and viewpoints of "the people," but engage in a broad dialogue with experts, politicians, people of faith or none, etc. Indeed, this kind of public theology would seek to facilitate a broad participation in the discussions on how to deal with ongoing climate change, inviting the participation of weak publics and seeking to make them strong publics.

Thirdly, a public theology of this kind would rely on some ethical principles—love, justice, reconciliation, and peace—but always ask how they should be applied in a given context and when faced with particular political issues. In response to climate change, it would seek to link the local and the global, articulate a responsibility to resist injustice and suggest practical ways of dealing with the crisis at hand. It would, however, refrain from identifying itself with the policies of particular political parties.

Finally, a kairotic public theology would also address how Christians, the church, and Christian theology are part of, contributing to, or victims of climate change. It would address theological controversies and reject theologies that contribute to the climate crisis and thus the suffering of all of creation. However, even within this kind of framework, public theologians might still end up with differing conclusions. This would reflect a Christian pluralism and the fact that the Bible, the Christian tradition, and Christian theology does not offer a blue print for political action, not even in times of climate change.

9

Responding to Crisis

In this final chapter I want to pull together the different threads from the preceding discussion and argue more systematically for a kairos inspired public theology. First I revisit the notion of a glocal public sphere and then the problems of social analysis, politics and ethics, and language and voice in public theology. In summary, I will argue that the task of public theology is one of interruption and imagination. I conclude that public theology, at its best, interrupts the debate and expands the imagination of the public sphere.

THE GLOCAL PUBLIC SPHERE

Habermas traced the origins of the modern public sphere to the bourgeois coffee houses and *salons* of the early Enlightenment. Even contemporary public theology is practiced in local settings: in cafés, restaurants, and community halls, and in face-to-face conversations with friends and acquaintances, neighbors, and fellow citizens. This is a reminder that public theology must be shaped and articulated in ways that makes sense and give meaning in such local interactions, and this is also its challenge. Venturing into specific relationships and concrete communities, public theology needs to be both informed by, and to engage with, such particular contexts. Public theology must be rooted in popular participation and the experienced living conditions in local contexts.

As the nation-state has become the political building block of the world order, the national context is also a key arena for political debates. Given the importance of this arena, it is not surprising that public theology addresses national issues. The difference in scale leads, however, to new tasks and challenges for public theology. The issues and concerns of public theology are broadened and the complexities involved become another challenge to the field. With globalization, the public sphere stretches even further and beyond both the local and the national realm. Today, public theology must be informed by people, matters, and concerns outside the comfortable boundaries of national borders, domestic debates, and particular communities. Consequently, the complexity of public theology is compounded.

Turning to the kairos documents, they reflect the local dimension of public theology in that they are popular documents that have come into being through broad participation of many actors. This applies in particular to the South African document. The process leading up to the publication of this document involved a large number of individuals and groups. The first drafts of the document were circulated in various groups, discussed, and revised. *The Road to Damascus* seems to have had a more limited genesis, in the sense that it to a larger extent is the product of a smaller group of dedicated clergy, theologians, activists, and others. The same applies to *Kairos Palestine*. Still, both *The Road to Damascus and Kairos Palestine* have a long list of signatories and insist that they represent and give voice to "the people." As noted, the documents also share an inductive and empirical approach in their analysis, with a strong focus on how the effects of social conflicts and policies impact on the everyday lives of ordinary people. The authors seem to share the experiences of the poor and marginalized and this is articulated as a cry of pain and call for change.

Regarding the other dimensions of the public sphere, the national context is most explicit in the case of *Kairos South Africa*, while a regional level is at the fore of *Kairos Palestine*. The conflict in the Middle-East and the Israeli occupation of Palestinian territories is the context and immediate background for this document. *The Road to Damascus* stands out as the most profoundly international document. It is authored and signed by a wide range of individuals from different parts of the world and the problems it addresses relate to international processes and relations: international politics, economics, division of labor etc. The document also calls on international society to respond to the social realities it describes and criticizes. This latter point is, however, something it shares with both *Kairos South Africa* and *Kairos Palestine*, and in this sense this international dimension can be considered a key trait of all of these three documents and of kairos theology.

These local, national, and global dimensions of the kairos documents reflect the character of the issues they address. South African apartheid was closely related to the specific history of the country (although racial discrimination could be found in other parts of the world), but the discourse on apartheid became a global discourse. Apartheid was perceived to contradict universal human rights, a policy that not only civil society groups but also states and governments could not remain indifferent to. Thus a global anti-apartheid campaign came about, a campaign that would eventually celebrate the release of Nelson Mandela, free elections, and the fall of apartheid in the early 1990s. Similarly, the current Israeli/Palestinian conflict is deeply contextual and local, though at the same time undoubtedly international and global in character.

This multi-layered feature of kairos theology not only reflects the issues, but also suggests how public theology can be produced and articulated in a glocal fashion when addressing contemporary crises. Indeed, the kairos documents are relatively short, well-considered, theological contributions that can be read, discussed, and reconsidered in the many different arenas of the glocal public sphere, including local civil society actors, non-governmental organizations, and social movements, as well as the movement of public opinion. They draw on the experiences and viewpoints of many and in particular the poor and marginalized. They also make seemingly local matters, global matters, address practical matters, mobilize support, and call for new forms of representation and solidarity in new public spheres. In this way, kairos theology suggests an innovative way of communicating in the public sphere: a glocal public theology that emerges in dialogue with local and national experiences and theologies, with scope and ambition to make itself known and relevant to a number of audiences in the glocal public sphere.

PUBLIC THEOLOGY AND SOCIAL ANALYSIS

In its widest sense, public theology is the sharing of theologically informed contributions in the public sphere and a continuous exercise that seeks to be relevant at all times and in many places. Thus, the social analysis and policy suggestions put forward by public theology are not given and will be different from place to place and from time to time. This indicates how the problem of social analysis—what theology should say about social issues—cannot be solved purely in the abstract, but must be discussed in relation to a given context and a particular challenge. Indeed, what public theology should say about social issues in times of crisis depends on the character of the crisis. However, kairos theology does point to some potential features of a contextually relevant social analysis in times of crisis.

The kairos documents emerge out of conflict ridden contexts where these documents and their authors see a crisis. In the South African document the authors describe a South Africa marked by "conflict, crisis and struggle" (KSA 4.1). Similarly, "the everyday reality of human sacrifice" (RD 58) is an important concern in *The Road to Damascus*, and *Kairos Palestine* responds to "oppression and occupation" (KP Introduction) and the "dead end in the tragedy of the Palestinian people" (KP Introduction). What the kairos authors see is an extraordinary reality: a tyrannical regime (KSA), structural oppression (RD), and occupation (KP) that is politically, morally, and theologically illegitimate. Kairos theology is contextual also in the sense that its methodology is inductive. The analysis goes from "the ground" and upwards, and focusses on the challenges, suffering, and every day experiences of the poor. Being rooted in, and concerned about, such political contexts and their social challenges is a characteristic of kairos theology.

The identification of conflict lines in society is another key feature of the Marxist inspired and conflict oriented social analysis. The socio-economic-political reality is considered a place of conflict. As Gerald West argues:

> it is this structural or systemic analysis of church and society that is the defining feature of *The Kairos Document* and all the 'kairos' documents that stand in its trajectory. This is what unites the various 'kairos' documents; a detailed socio-historical structural analysis determined by each specific context.[1]

This structural analysis leads the kairos authors to identify a number of conflicts in society that are unjust and oppressive. This is reflected in the strong normative assessment of the status quo and a call to change the given social, economic, and political circumstances. Thus, the hermeneutics

---

1. West, "Tracing the 'Kairos' Trajectory," 20, original emphasis.

and social analysis aim not only at understanding or describing "what is happening." They also have a normative ambition to change society.

West also distinguishes between people's theology and prophetic theology, arguing that people's theology is the process while the prophetic theology is the product of kairos theology. He writes that the:

> theological process is a significant and distinctive feature of the South African *Kairos Document*. This theological process has a distinctive shape, beginning with people's theology and then moving to prophetic theology, all within the overall shape of a 'See—Judge—Act' methodological process.[2]

This particular and contextual feature of the kairos documents is thus closely related to their theological character. They draw on classic theological sources—the Bible and the Christian tradition—and they go into a discussion with various forms of theological thinking. A key concern is to reject forms of theological thinking that the authors find it necessary to warn against, reject, and denounce. In fact, the analysis is theologically informed from the outset, and facilitates a theological reflection on social issues. The interest of kairos theology lies thus not in the relationship between faith and unbelief, but between different types of faith and their socio-economic-political implications.

In other words, kairos theology is not abstract theology. In fact, the use of abstract concepts to describe the current situation is explicitly rejected. Rather, kairos theology relies on a social analysis of a given situation and is characterized by a specific method that combines theology and social theory. This approach makes kairos theology an interdisciplinary undertaking. The social analysis is dependent on the integration of perspectives and insights from both the social sciences and Christian theology, and in bringing together such perspectives and integrating them into one combined analysis with normative implications, kairos theology adopts, as noted by West, liberation theology's three-step-approach: social analysis (see), reflection on the social realities (judge) and the response to these realities through practical action (act). This also represents a strong rejection of any perceived abyss between the social sciences on the one hand, and theology on the other hand.

It is noteworthy, however, that although the normative and political commitment is strong, the kairos documents stress that they have a

---

2. Ibid., 14–15, original emphasis.

tentative character. The South African document explicitly states it is "an open-ended document which will never be said to be final" and presents itself as "a beginning, a platform for further discussion" (KSA, preface to the first edition). The reader is promised that further editions will follow and in the second edition the authors write that "there is nothing final about this document not even about this second edition" (KSA, conclusion). Similarly, in *The Road to Damascus* the authors are committed to engage in self-criticism. They write: "We are all in continuous need of self-criticism and conversion" (RD, preamble) and "need to search our own hearts for remnants of the same sins" (RD 91). The sharp criticism is, in other words, not a one-sided criticism but also a source of self-criticism: "Instead of working for justice and liberation, we have often remained uninvolved" (RD 44).

Although acknowledging their short-comings, this does not prevent the kairos authors from addressing suffering and injustices they are witnessing: "Although we are conscious of our own sins, we must raise our voice in the denunciation of this sin. It is a sin that serves total war being waged against the people, leading to the death and destruction of our communities" (RD 47). This makes kairos theology not one specific and fixed theology, and suggests a dynamic approach in public theology that constantly revisits its own analysis, arguments, and conclusions, and invites others to do the same.

Only to a limited extent, however, do these documents self-critically discuss how kairos theology is a reflection of its social context. The extent to which kairos theology relies on other, implicit or explicit, factors in its social context that define or shape this kind of theology in an implied or unreflected manner, needs closer consideration. One obvious question, is: Does its context and social analysis shape or frame the theological outlook in an (il)legitimate way? Although kairos theology hardly answers this question, it is a task public theology must acknowledge and make its own.

Still, kairos theology suggests that the social analysis of public theology should seek to be informed by knowledge and insights from a wide range of academic fields, in particular theology and the social sciences, and to give informed and constructive contributions to the ongoing discussions in the public sphere. Similarly, public theology should reflect critically on context and conflicts and see God as involved in these conflicts on the side of the poor and oppressed. By offering this kind of (self-)critical and creative social analysis, public theology can give a unique and important contribution in times of crisis.

PUBLIC THEOLOGY, POLITICS, AND ETHICS

The public sphere is a pluralistic arena for discursive exchange. In this arena people come together to discuss their concerns, visions, and hopes. Still, the critique from Nancy Frazer and others of Habermas' notion of the public sphere is immensely important to public theology. The public sphere cuts across the cultural, religious, political, and socio-economic divides in society, but does not eliminate these differences. The ability to participate in the public sphere continues to vary from individual to individual and group to group. Such differences, and any restrictions on the public sphere, contradict the egalitarian theological notion that all men and women are created equal and in the image of God. It is not the open character of the public sphere, but any restrictions placed on it that need justification. The restrictions Nancy Frazer and others have pointed out do not carry such justification, are illegitimate, and should therefore be challenged and defeated.

The kairos documents suggest how public theology can articulate this task of inclusivity. In the mid-1980s the South African kairos document not only articulated a radical criticism of the status quo, it also demanded an open, free, and inclusive public sphere and "laid the foundations for the theology of a transition that led to the debates about justice, reparation and reconciliation."[3] Similarly, *Kairos Palestine* is a contribution determined by the will to work for collaboration and peace. Its universal and inclusive perspective determines the analysis and the invitation to dialogue and cooperation. The belief in a good God, hope, and universal love establishes a common platform that can be shared across political and religious divides.[4]

In this way, the kairos authors acknowledge that there can be conflict between religion and politics and address religious interpretations that contribute to human suffering and maintain the status quo of oppression and injustice. Consequently, they argue explicitly against certain types of religion and denounce others' interpretation of Christian theology. Accordingly, the kairos documents illustrate the role religion can play as a critical and constructive partner in public discourse. The moral commitment to justice and concern for human suffering are used in the document

---

3. De Gruchy, "From Political to Public Theologies," 52.
4. Fretheim, "Power of Invitation."

as critical resources to assess religious traditions and interpretations. Similarly, politics and policies are critically assessed from a religious point of view.

As religion and politics are viewed neither as separate nor incompatible, the way they are integrated in kairos theology calls not only for an interdisciplinary approach to social issues in times of crisis, but also for political and moral action. The readers are called to act to make the world a better place for all and in particular for the poor and marginalized. This involves a rejection of the notion that Christians are called to obedience towards political authorities, as well as the notion that Christian virtues are independent of any social analysis. Indeed, the kairos documents criticize an overly abstract approach in Christian ethics and Christian political involvement. In contrast, kairos theology highlights the necessity of justice for reconciliation to happen as a "true reconciliation." They also underline how love should be a guiding principle in all the actions of churches and Christians.

The call for action is substantiated through the specification of concrete actions and policies that the documents recommend, thus answering the key question implied in the problem of politics and ethics: what kind of political and moral actions should public theology recommend? In the kairos documents this includes for example boycott and divestment, and in some cases (though not all) the use of violence. In this way, kairos theology contrasts with an individualized or privatized form of Christian theology and ethics. Kairos theology thus also contrasts with the framework for doing theology developed by Robert Benne. While Benne focuses on the core vision of the Church and narrows this down to doctrinal issues and, in some exceptional cases, moral or political issues, the latter are, in kairos theology, seen as an integral part of Christian theology.

Kairos theology also contrasts with the middle axiom approach in that it adopts a critical attitude towards compromise and highlights a visionary, and to a large extent idealistic, approach to Christian political involvement. At the same time, they stress the realistic dimensions of political involvement. In this sense, kairos theology seems to balance the idealism and realism of Christian ethics in a different way from Christian realism and the middle-axiom approach. This relates to how suffering and oppression are a starting point, but not the end of kairos theology. Rather, the kairos documents close with a message of hope. The documents have a positive tone and eschatological vision that sets the agenda for practical action.

In this way, the kairos documents blur conventional distinctions such as theology and social science, the political, the religious, and the ethical. The authors combine these categories in a fluid and dynamic manner, where one cannot easily be distinguished from the other. Religious or moral commitment is not limited to a religious or distinct, separate social sphere. Similarly, the kairos authors undoubtedly have a political agenda, but do not leave their faith and religious outlook behind when entering the public realm to engage in political and policy related discourses in a creative and innovative fashion. Neither do they commit themselves to one particular political ideology or system.

These features of kairos theology suggest that public theology should not remain within the realm of ideal theory, but be committed to contributing to real life public exchange. Public theology should seek not only to contribute to debates in the public sphere for the sake of discussion and complementary learning, but also to improve the public sphere and political decision making. The task of public theology is neither to control the public sphere nor to take the moral high ground in its ongoing discussions on social issues. Public theology should, however, seek to constructively open up and shape the public sphere in an inclusive manner and with a special preference for the poor, oppressed, and marginalized.

Further, this preferential option for the poor is the basis for the challenge to take action. The "option for the poor" demands that public theology approaches history from the perspective of those who suffer the most. The poor and marginalized become the hermeneutical lens and criterion though which to judge all social progress. This perspective defines the outlook of public theology and how it analyzes society and seeks to change it.

Informed by policy dilemmas and committed to the well-being of all and the poor and marginalized in particular, public theology should seek to provide both critical and constructive policy recommendations. Public theology should suggest how individuals, groups, churches, and others should act in times of crisis. Such suggestions would substantiate and clarify the normative dimensions of the social analysis and spell out its practical implications. In doing this, public theology will be marked by a fair degree of idealism, an equal amount of realism as well as a relentless insistence on hope in times of oppression, suffering, and crisis. Given the participatory, contextual, and tentative character of public theology, these policy recommendations must be understood as considered suggestions that need to be revised and reconsidered over time and from context to context. Public theology's policy suggestions should not close the debate, but open it, specify it, and hopefully improve it.

PUBLIC THEOLOGY, LANGUAGE, AND VOICE

Seeking to give a contextually theologically informed contribution to the public sphere, public theology seeks to develop a language that is an authentic Christian witness, but also widely accessible, even to those with little or no knowledge of the Christian faith. Contributing, communicating, and making oneself understood in the public sphere can be challenging, in particular if one seeks to communicate with a wide range of different audiences in the glocal public sphere. Success depends not only on the character of the public sphere and its participants, but also on how one chooses to express oneself. This is the problem of language and voice in public theology.

Any approach to this issue must acknowledge that the public sphere is the communal space where people meet, live, and share their experiences, views, and opinions. This multifaceted public space is based on a minimum of shared rationality and ethics often described as a universal and secular rationality, but this has been challenged for different reasons. First, the notion of a universal rationality is challenged by the postmodern emphasis on, and celebration of, the plurality of narratives and rationalities. Second, the notion of a secular rationality seems to exclude religious approaches and thus also religiously informed contributions to the public sphere.

Against this background, Habermas' later understanding of the relationship between religion and the public sphere seems sound and constructive. Rather than seeing religious contributions as foreign to the public sphere, they should be welcomed as part of the open conversation. Not only will this be the preferred language of some, but there might also be unique perspectives and interpretations that thus can be made available and accessible to others. This requires a willingness to listen and to learn, an open attitude that welcomes the voice, concerns, and experiences of others as not exclusively theirs, but also mine and ours. Habermas' position thus welcomes a kind of public theology which is explicit about its Christian roots and outlook. It is open for theological contributions in the public conversation.

In kairos theology references to the Christian faith and the Bible are abundant. The kairos documents refer to, and quote, the Bible and make extensive use of biblical language and rhetoric. In addition, there is ample use of theological terminology. Indeed, kairos theology combines different kinds of languages, theological moods, and discourses, and thus creates its own hybrid, kairos language. This hybrid language contrasts kairos theology with approaches that seek to exclude any kind of religious language in the public sphere, but equally to fundamentalist or apologetic approaches that primarily rely on the language of faith.

The many different languages and voices heard in the kairos documents can be seen as a combination of different discourses that appeal to different audiences and that interpret each other. One advantage of this is shown, for example, by how Palestine is referred to as a Holy Land. Here religious terminology is actively used to reinterpret the meaning of the Holy Land and its political implications. The kairos authors see "the land" as a promise of peace and justice for all, thus giving a new interpretation of the conflict at hand. In such ways, religious language is not necessarily a conversation-stopper, but rather a tool that enables new understandings, interpretations, and visions.

The kairos documents not only use biblical language but also feature a large degree of trust in the Bible. As Gerald West has pointed out, the South African kairos document was written "by 'the people', for whom the Bible was/is predominantly a site of trust, not suspicion, this meant that it became a primary (and substantially an unproblematic) source for doing 'kairos' theology."[5] This hermeneutics of trust contrasts kairos theology with important strands within liberation theology, notably feminist and South African Black theology.[6] As West writes, a:

> recognition of contending trajectories in the Bible would have been of use, for example, to *Kairos Palestine* in its engagement with contending biblical interpretations around the land issue. Labelling a form of biblical interpretation "fundamentalist," as *Kairos Palestine* does, or claiming, as the [South African] Kairos document does, that the biblical interpretations of the apartheid state are either "misusing" the Bible or have "no biblical foundation" is to delay dealing with a deeply ambiguous Bible.[7]

This kind of hermeneutics of suspicion is not articulated in the kairos documents; neither is a reflection on the ambiguity of biblical texts on issues such as conflict, war, violence, power etc.

5. West, "Tracing the 'Kairos' Trajectory," 21.
6. Ibid., 19.
7. Ibid., 21–22.

On the other hand, the kairos documents do discuss key hermeneutical principles for reading such texts, including the need for a critical distance to the text, its current application, and practical implications. As West also highlights, the structural analysis that is common to the kairos documents, as well as the clear contrasting and denouncing of alternative theologies, to some extent compensates for their lack of biblical criticism. In this sense, kairos theology is characterized by social, political, and theological criticism rather than biblical criticism. Rather than a biblical hermeneutics of suspicion there is a socio-theological hermeneutics of suspicion that characterizes this approach. Similarly, the Word of God is seen as dynamic and fluent, always recognized by its commitment to the poor and marginalized.

In this way, kairos theology suggests a creative and imaginative language and voice for public theology. The use of religious language in the public sphere might surprise or provoke, but can also pave the way for a learning opportunity. By combining the particular language of the Christian tradition with rational and secular language, and integrating them closely in one and the same analysis, they can become more than parallel accounts. They interpret and inform each other, creating a room for new interpretations of social, political, and theological issues and new visions for a common future.

INTERRUPTION AND IMAGINATION

To sum up, kairos theology shows how public theology can contribute with an innovative kind of social analysis, constructive policy suggestions, and a creative language in the public sphere. Public theology can give a new and different voice to the voiceless, the suffering poor, the oppressed, and marginalized, and challenge the dynamics of the public sphere when concerns for the poor are disregarded and their voices are excluded.

This feature of public theology can be described as one of *interruption*. This is not the same as disruption. Violence disrupts normal life in the village, but a question to the speaker or an ambulance driving by does not bring the lecture or the conversations in the street to a halt. They interrupt and disturb, but they do not destroy. A public theology that interrupts does not disrupt or destroy the public discussions, but it challenges its assumptions and direction with novel viewpoints and thought provoking perspectives. At times this can be done in a mild, reform oriented, and realistic way, for example along the lines of Niebuhrian realism and the middle axiom approach. At other times such interruptions will be need to be revolutionary, visionary, or utopian, for example as is often the case in liberationist contributions to public debate.

Further, kairos theology suggests how public theology not only can interrupt, but by introducing new perspectives, hybrid language, and a range of different discourses it can expand the *imagination* of the public sphere. The relationship between theology and sociology is often described as one of conflict, but in the kairos documents they merge. This combination of sociology and theology, as well as ethics, can be immensely productive. Indeed, one way of describing sociology and theology is to see them as different forms of imagination: the capacity to sees "beyond the empirical" and "supplements what reason observes, thus disclosing a richer vision of reality."[8]

For C. Wright Mills, who coined the term "sociological imagination," the task of sociology was to help one to understand broader, social processes in which an individual biography is involved.[9] Similarly, the task of theology is to help one to interpret the world we live in, in light of the Christian faith. Theological imagination invites one to see social issues and current crises in light of the Christian understanding of God who created heaven and earth, Jesus Christ who shared the suffering of the world, and The Holy Spirit who is present among us and keeps faith alive. Further, this is a prophetic imagination with the ability to "*nurture, nourish, and evoke a consciousness and perception alternative to the consciousness and perception of the dominant culture around us.*"[10]

By drawing on both kinds of imagination, public theology can seek to put religious resources into circulation and encourage creativity and unconventional thinking, thus expanding the imagination of the public sphere. In this way it moves beyond both a pure idealism and pragmatic realism, and becomes constructionist. In the same way that social constructionism[11] emphasizes the role of language and language use, the production of meaning through human interaction and the meaning of reality for different people in different locations, constructionist public theology

---

8. McGrath, *Mere Theology*, drawing on Murdoch, "The Darkness of Practical Reason."

9. Mills, *Sociological Imagination*.

10. Brueggemann, *Prophetic Imagination*, 3, original emphasis.

11. Parker, *Social Constructionism*, and Gergen, *Invitation to Social Construction*.

focuses on popular participation, the construction of meaning, and shared understanding of social issues and shared challenges.

As William Cavanaugh points out in the introduction to his book *Theopolitical Imagination*: "Politics is a practice of the imagination. Sometimes politics is 'the art of the possible,' but it is always an art, and engages the imagination just as art does."[12] A kairos inspired public theology could offer new and alternative concepts, perspectives, and interpretations—resources that could suggest different discourses and an imaginative reading of the crisis and challenges at hand.

In times of crisis and in the twenty-first century, public debate needs this kind of innovative social analysis, creative policy proposals, and hybrid language. With this kind of approach public theology can interrupt the current affairs of the public sphere, and invite its participants and audiences to expand their imagination with respect not only to the future utopia of the world, but also with regard to specific actions and policies. At its best, a public theology will do both: interrupt and imagine, to the benefit of all who will listen and learn.

12. Cavanaugh, *Theopolitical Imagination*, 1.

Conclusion

Christian theology is much more than doctrinal deliberations. Theology is the study of the meaning of Christian faith and its implications for individuals and groups in the contemporary world. To fulfill this task, theology cannot disregard society, but it must reflect on, and seek to understand, society. Given the current crises—the oppression, injustice, and suffering of our time—theology must also seek to change society. Theology should not be reduced to abstract God-talk, but involve social analysis and political involvement. Public theology takes this task into the public sphere and engages in dialogue and debate with representatives of a wider range of groups and individuals in "the larger society." It brings Christian faith and perspectives to the public sphere and seeks to contribute constructively to the public debate and to address the challenges of the day.

Public theology thus relates to the specific issues, challenges, and languages of the context within which it speaks. This feature of public theology places it in the liminal position between church and public life, which Graham refers to as the place between a rock and a hard place[1] whilst Kim describes it as a "struggle between the tension of keeping Christian distinctiveness and creating a shared platform for a common conversation."[2] From this perspective and in order to respond to the complex realities and diverse interpretations of the world we live in and the challenges people face, public theology needs to be glocal. It needs to be conscious of, informed by, and in constant interaction with the global public sphere as well as the specific local contexts.

In this book I have argued how a public theology inspired by the kairos documents links the local experience of poverty, injustice, and oppression

1. Graham, *Between a Rock and a Hard Place*.
2. Kim, *Theology in the Public Sphere*, 25.

with national and global structures of financial and political power. It expounds a social analysis that is as theological as it is sociological, combining and merging perspectives in one and the same analysis. Kairos inspired public theology identifies and highlights theological controversies, social conflict, and oppressive structures. Whoever and whatever legitimizes or justifies such conflicts and their related suffering are criticized, denounced, and called to repent. It offers policy suggestions and specific moral actions, calls for a new and better world, but also acknowledges the dilemmas of policy making. Some forms of compromise are rejected, while others are accepted according to the specific character of the crisis at hand.

Through its social analysis, political and ethical recommendations, language, and voice, this kind of public theology seeks to critically interrupt the public debate and constructively expand the imagination of its participants. In all of this, however, this kind of public theology remains self-critical and invites feed-back, alternative suggestions and different perspectives from its conversation partners in the public sphere. It offers concrete recommendations, but acknowledges the contextual, preliminary, and particular character of any social analysis and its related policy suggestions.

To fulfil this task the public theologian can be understood as a connected critic[3] or an organic intellectual.[4] She is intimately connected to the society, the issues, and, the people of her context, but seeks, through critical loyalty, to disclose the social processes and conflicts that result in oppression, injustice, and suffering. She shares and articulates the pain of those who suffer oppression and injustice, the poor and marginalized and she denounces those who legitimize the status quo, calling for radical social change and hopes for a better future. This idealistic, radical, and prophetic language is, however, combined with a realistic, reform oriented and pragmatic approach, combining religious and secular language in one and the same analysis.

All of this makes public theology in times of crisis a creative and constructive undertaking. It seeks not only to criticize policies and politicians, but also to suggest ways forward. It contributes with a new language and innovative perspectives suggestions for solutions to the issues, concerns, and crisis at hand. Public theology is neither exclusively idealistic nor exclusively realistic, but suggests and invites new perspectives, insights, and interpretations to inform the public debate. In this sense, a kairos inspired

---

3. Thiemann, "Public Theologian."
4. Gramsci, *Selections from Prison Notebooks*, 6.

Conclusion

public theology is a constructionist public theology. It seeks new and shared understanding in the public sphere and a complementary learning process about the social issues and challenges at hand.

Bibliography

Adams, Nicholas. *Habermas and Theology*. Cambridge: Cambridge University Press, 2006.
Aguilar, Mario I. "Public Theology from the Periphery: Victims and Theologians." *International Journal of Public Theology* 1 (2007) 321–37.
Amin, Samir. *Accumulation on a World Scale: A Critique of the Theory of Underdevelopment*. New York: Monthly Review, 1974.
Amirtham, Samuel, and John S. Pobee. *Theology by the People: Reflections on Doing Theology in Community*. Geneva: World Council of Churches, 1986.
Anderson, Benedict. *Imagined Communities: Reflections on the Origin and Spread of Nationalism*. Rev. 3rd ed. London: Verso, 2006.
Astley, Jeff, and Leslie J. Francis. *Exploring Ordinary Theology: Everyday Christian Believing and the Church*. Farnham: Ashgate, 2013.
Ateek, Naim Stifan. *Justice, and Only Justice: A Palestinian Theology of Liberation*. Maryknoll, NY: Orbis, 1989.
———. *A Palestinian Christian Cry for Reconciliation*. Maryknoll, NY: Orbis, 2008.
Atherton, John. "Marginalisation, Manchester and the Scope of Public Theology." In *The Future of Christian Social Ethics: Essays on the Work of Ronald H. Preston 1913-2001*, edited by Elaine L. Graham and Esther D. Reed, 20–36. London: Continuum, 2004.
———. *Public Theology for Changing Times*. London: SPCK, 2000.
Audi, Robert, and Nicholas Wolterstorff. *Religion in the Public Square: The Place of Religious Convictions in Political Debate*. Lanham, MD: Rowman & Littlefield, 1997.
Augustine. *The Confessions; the City of God; On Christian Doctrine*. Edited by Mortimer J. Adler. Chicago: Encyclopedia Britannica, 1990.
Barkat, Anwar M., and James Mutmabirwa, eds. *Challenge to the Church: A Theological Comment on the Political Crisis in South Africa. The Kairos Dokument and Commentaries*. Geneva: World Council of Churches, 1985.
Barnes, Michael Horace. *Theology and the Social Sciences*. Lanham, MD: University Press of America, 2001.
Baum, Gregory. "The Theological Method of Segundo's *the Liberation of Theology*." In *Proceedings of the Catholic Theological Society of America*, edited by Catholic Theological Society of America, 120–24. Milwaukee: Catholic Theological Society of America, 1977.
Bauman, Zygmunt. *Globalization: The Human Consequences*. Cambridge: Polity, 1998.
———. *Liquid Modernity*. Cambridge: Polity, 2000.
Beck, Ulrich. *Risk Society: Towards a New Modernity*. Translated by Mark Rittter. London: Sage, 1992.

Bibliography

———. *What Is Globalization?* Translated by Patrick Camiller. Cambridge: Polity, 2000.
Bedford-Strohm, Heinrich. "Poverty and Public Theology: Advocacy of the Church in Pluralistic Society." *International Journal of Public Theology* 2 (2008) 144–62.
———. "Public Theology and Political Ethics." *International Journal of Public Theology* 6 (2012) 273–91.
———. "Public Theology and the Global Economy. Ecumenical Social Thinking between Fundamental Criticism and Reform." *DDEEL* 48 (2007) 8–24.
———. "Public Theology of Ecology and Civil Society." In *Religion and Ecology in the Public Sphere*, edited by Celia Deane-Drummond and Heinrich Bedford-Strohm, 39–56. New York: T. & T. Clark, 2011.
Bedford-Strohm, Heinrich, and Celia Deane-Drummond. *Religion and Ecology in the Public Sphere*. London: T. & T. Clark, 2011.
Benne, Robert. *The Paradoxical Vision: A Public Theology for the Twenty-First Century*. Minneapolis: Fortress, 1995.
Berger, Peter L. *The Sacred Canopy: Elements of a Sociological Theory of Religion*. New York: Anchor/Doubleday, 1969.
Berger, Peter L., and Thomas Luckmann. *The Social Construction of Reality: A Treatise in the Sociology of Knowledge*. Garden City, NY: Anchor/Doubleday, 1967.
Bergmann, Sigurd. *God in Context: A Survey of Contextual Theology*. Aldershot: Ashgate, 2003.
Bevans, Stephen B. *Models of Contextual Theology*. Maryknoll, NY: Orbis, 2002.
Biggar, Nigel. *Behaving in Public: How to Do Christian Ethics*. Grand Rapids: Eerdmans, 2011.
Boff, Leonardo, and Clodovis Boff. *Introducing Liberation Theology*. Translated by Paul Burns. Tunbridge Wells: Burns & Oates, 1987.
Bonhoeffer, Dietrich. *Ethics*. Translated by Neville Horton Smith. New York: Touchstone, 1995.
Breitenberg, E. Harold, Jr. "To Tell the Truth: Will the Real Public Theology Please Stand Up?" *Journal of the Society of Christian Ethics* 23 (2003) 55–96.
Brewer, John D. "Sociology and Theology Reconsidered: Religious Sociology and the Sociology of Religion in Britain." *History of the Human Sciences* 20 (2007) 7–28.
Brown, Robert McAfee, ed. *Kairos: Three Prophetic Challenges to the Church*. Grand Rapids: Eerdmans, 1990.
Bruce, Steve. *Secularization: In Defence of an Unfashionable Theory*. Oxford: Oxford University Press, 2011.
Brueggemann, Walter. *The Land: Place as Gift, Promise, and Challenge in Biblical Faith*. Philadelphia: Fortress, 1977.
———. *The Prophetic Imagination*. 2nd ed. Minneapolis: Fortress, 2001.
Brundtland, Gro Harlem. "Our Common Future." Oxford: Oxford University Press, 1987.
Burdziej, Stanislaw. "Sociological and Theological Imagination in a Post-Secular Society." *Polish Sociological Review* 2 (2014) 179–93.
Burge, Gary M. *Jesus and the Land: The New Testament Challenge to "Holy Land" Theology*. Grand Rapids: Baker Academic, 2010.
———. *Whose Land? Whose Promise? What Christians Are Not Being Told About Israel and the Palestinians*. Cleveland: Pilgrim, 2003.
Butler, Judith. *Precarious Life: The Powers of Mourning and Violence*. New York: Verso, 2004.

Bibliography

Butler, Judith, Eduardo Mendieta, and Jonathan Van Antwerpen. *The Power of Religion in the Public Sphere*. New York: Columbia University Press, 2011.

Buttelli, Felibe Gustavo Koch. "Public Theology as Theology on Kairos: The South African *Kairos Document* as a Model of Public Theology." *Journal of Theology for Southern Africa* (2012) 90–106.

Cahill, Lisa Sowle. *Theological Bioethics: Participation, Justice, and Change*. Washington, DC: Georgetown University Press, 2005.

Calhoun, Craig J., ed. *Habermas and the Public Sphere*. Cambridge, MA: MIT Press, 1992.

Calhoun, Craig, Eduardo Mendieta, and Jonathan Van Antwerpen. *Habermas and Religion*. Cambridge: Polity, 2013.

Carson, Rachel. *Silent Spring*. London: Hamish Hamilton, 1963.

Casanova, José. *Public Religions in the Modern World*. Chicago: University of Chicago Press, 1994.

Castells, Manuel. "The New Public Sphere: Global Civil Society, Communication Networks and Global Governance." *ANNALS AAPSS* 616 (2008) 78–93.

Catholic Institute for International Relations. *The Kairos Document: A Theological Comment on the Political Crisis in South Africa*. Catholic Institute for International Relations (CIIR) and British Council of Churches (BCC), 1986.

———. *The Road to Damascus: Kairos and Conversion*. Catholic Institute for International Relations (CIIR) and Christian Aid, 1990.

Cavanaugh, William. *Theopolitical Imagination: Christian Practices of Space and Time*. New York: T. & T. Clark, 2002.

Chapman, Colin. *Whose Promised Land? The Continuing Crisis over Israel and Palestine*. Oxford: Lion, 2002.

Chopp, Rebecca S. *The Power to Speak: Feminism, Language, God*. Eugene, OR: Wipf & Stock, 2002.

Church of Sweden. "A Bishops' Letter About the Climate." Uppsala: The Swedish Church, 2014.

Cobb, John B., Jr. *Is It Too Late? A Theology of Ecology*. New York: Bruce, 1972.

Cochrane, James R. "Against the Grain: Responsible Public Theology in a Global Era." *International Journal of Public Theology* 5 (2011) 44–62.

Cone, James H. *A Black Theology of Liberation*. Philadelphia: Lippincott, 1970.

Cooper, Thia. *The Reemergence of Liberation Theologies: Models for the Twenty-First Century*. Basingstoke: Palgrave Macmillan, 2013.

Critchley, Simon. *The Faith of the Faithless: Experiments in Political Theology*. London: Verso, 2012.

Davies, W. D. *The Gospel and the Land*. Berkeley: University of California Press, 1974.

De Gruchy, John W. "From Political to Public Theologies: The Role of Theology in Public Life in South Africa." In *Public Theology for the 21st Century: Essays in Honour of Duncan B. Forrester*, edited by William F. Storrar and Andrew R. Morton, 45–62. London: T. & T. Clark, 2004.

———. "Public Theology as Christian Witness: Exploring the Genre." *International Journal of Public Theology* 1 (2007) 26–41.

Deane-Drummond, Celia. *Eco-Theology*. London: Darton, Longman and Todd, 2008.

Dussel, Enrique D. "The Sociohistorical Meaning of Liberation Theology (Reflections About Its Origin and World Context)." In *Religions/Globalizations: Theories and Cases*, edited by Dwight N. Hopkins et al., 33–45. Durham: Duke University Press, 2001.

Bibliography

Eisenstadt, S. N. "Comparative Civilizations and Multiple Modernities." Leiden: Brill, 2003.
Eriksen, Thomas Hylland. "Globalization: The Key Concepts." Oxford: Berg, 2007.
Feagin, Joe R., and Hernán Vera. *Liberation Sociology*. Boulder, CO: Westview, 2001.
Fiorenza, Francis Schüssler, Klaus Tanner, and Michael Welker, eds. *Political Theology: Contemporary Challenges and Future Directions*. Louisville: Westminster John Knox, 2013.
Ford, David. *The Future of Christian Theology*. Malden, MA: Wiley-Blackwell, 2011.
———. *Theology: A Very Short Introduction*. Oxford: Oxford University Press, 2000.
Forrester, Duncan B. *Christian Justice and Public Policy*. Cambridge: Cambridge University Press, 1997.
———. "The Scope of Public Theology." In *The Future of Christian Social Ethics: Essays on the Work of Ronald H. Preston 1913-2001*, edited by Elaine L. Graham and Esther D. Reed, 5-19. London: Continuum, 2004.
———. *Truthful Action: Explorations in Practical Theology*. Edinburgh: T. & T. Clark, 2000.
Foucault, Michel. *Discipline and Punish: The Birth of the Prison*. Translated by Alan Sheridan. London: Penguin, 1977.
Francis, of Assisi. "Canticle of the Creatures." In *Francis of Assisi: Early Documents*, edited by Regis J. Armstrong et al., 1:113-14. New York: New City, 1999.
Fraser, Nancy. "Rethinking the Public Sphere: A Contribution to the Critique of Actually Existing Democracy." *Social Text* (1990) 56-80.
Frei, Hans W., George Hunsinger, and William C. Placher. *Types of Christian Theology*. New Haven, CT: Yale University Press, 1992.
Fretheim, Kjetil. "The Power of Invitation: The Moral Discourse of *Kairos Palestine*." *Dialog* 51 (2012) 135-43.
Fukuyama, Francis. *The End of History and the Last Man*. London: Penguin, 1992.
Furseth, Inger, and Pål Repstad. *An Introduction to the Sociology of Religion: Classical and Contemporary Perspectives*. Aldershot: Ashgate, 2006.
Gellner, Ernest. *Nations and Nationalism*. Oxford: Blackwell, 1983.
Gergen, Kenneth J. *An Invitation to Social Construction*. 2nd ed. Los Angeles: SAGE, 2009.
Giddens, Anthony. *The Politics of Climate Change*. 2nd ed., rev. and updated. Cambridge: Polity, 2011.
Gill, Robin. *The Social Context of Theology: A Methodological Enquiry*. London: Mowbrays, 1975.
———. *Sociological Theology*. Farnham: Ashgate, 2012.
———. *Theology and Sociology: A Reader*. London: Cassell, 1996.
Goode, Luke. *Jürgen Habermas: Democracy and the Public Sphere*. London: Pluto, 2005.
Graham, Elaine. *Between a Rock and a Hard Place: Public Theology in a Post-Secular Age*. London: SCM, 2013.
Graham, Elaine L. "Guest Editorial." In *The Future of Christian Social Ethics: Essays on the Work of Ronald H. Preston, 1913-2001*, edited by Elaine L. Graham and Esther D. Reed, 1-4. London: Continuum, 2004.
Graham, Elaine L., and Esther D. Reed, eds. *The Future of Christian Social Ethics: Essays on the Work of Ronald H. Preston, 1913-2001*. London: Continuum, 2004.
Gramsci, Antonio. *Selections from Prison Notebooks*. London: Lawrence and Wishart, 1971.

Bibliography

Gripsrud, Jostein, et al., eds. *The Idea of the Public Sphere: A Reader.* Lanham, MD: Lexington, 2010.

Gushee, David P. *In the Fray: Contesting Christian Public Ethics, 1994-2013.* Eugene, OR: Cascade, 2014.

Gustafson, James M. "Varieties of Moral Discourse: Prophetic, Narrative, Ethical, and Policy." In *Seeking Understanding: The Stob Lectures, 1986-1998,* 43-76. Grand Rapids: Eerdmans, 2001.

Gutiérrez, Gustavo. *A Theology of Liberation: History, Politics, and Salvation.* London: SCM, 1988.

Habel, Norman C. *The Land Is Mine: Six Biblical Land Ideologies.* Minneapolis: Fortress, 1995.

Habel, Norman C., and Peter L. Trudinger. *Exploring Ecological Hermeneutics.* Atlanta: Scholars, 2008.

Habermas, Jürgen. *Between Facts and Norms: Contributions to a Discourse Theory of Law and Democracy.* Translated by William Reigh. Cambridge, MA: MIT Press, 1996.

———. *Between Naturalism and Religion: Philosophical Essays.* Translated by Ciaran Cronin. Cambridge: Polity, 2008.

———. "Notes on Post-Secular Society." *New Perspectives Quarterly* 5 (2008) 17-29.

———. *The Structural Transformation of the Public Sphere: Inquiry into a Category of Bourgeois Society.* Translated by Thomas Burger and Frederick Lawrence. Cambridge: Polity, 1992.

Hainsworth, Deidre King, and Scott R. Paeth, eds. *Public Theology for a Global Society: Essays in Honor of Max L. Stackhouse.* Grand Rapids: Eerdmans, 2010.

Hauerwas, Stanley. *After Christendom? How the Church Is to Behave If Freedom, Justice, and a Christian Nation Are Bad Ideas.* Nashville: Abingdon, 1991.

———. *In Good Company: Church as Polis.* Notre Dame: Notre Dame University Press, 1997.

———. "On Keeping Theological Ethics Theological." In *Revisions: Changing Perspectives in Moral Philosophy,* edited by Stanley Hauerwas and Alasdair MacIntyre, 16-42. Notre Dame: Notre Dame University Press, 1983.

———. *Truthfulness and Tragedy: Further Investigations in Christian Ethics.* Notre Dame: Notre Dame University Press, 1977.

Held, David, and Anthony G. McGrew. *Globalization/Anti-Globalization: Beyond the Great Divide.* London: Polity, 2007.

Herrmann, Wilhelm. *Ethik.* Tübingen: Mohr, 1913.

Hogue, Michael S. "After the Secular: Toward a Pragmatic Public Theology." *Journal of the American Academy of Religion* 78 (2010) 346-74.

Hollenbach, David. *The Common Good and Christian Ethics.* Cambridge: Cambridge University Press, 2002.

Hovey, Craig, William T. Cavanaugh, and Jeffrey W. Bailey. *An Eerdmans Reader in Contemporary Political Theology.* Grand Rapids: Eerdmans, 2012.

Huber, Wolfgang. *Kirche Und Öffentlichkeit.* E. Klett, 1973.

Hulme, Mike. *Why We Disagree About Climate Change.* Cambridge: Cambridge University Press, 2009.

Jacobsen, Eneida. "Models of Public Theology." *International Journal of Public Theology* 6 (2012) 7-22.

Jenkins, Willis. *The Future of Ethics: Sustainability, Social Justice, and Religious Creativity.* Washington, DC: Georgetown University Press, 2013.

Bibliography

Kairos Palestine. *A Moment of Truth: A Word of Faith, Hope, and Love from the Heart of Palestinian Suffering*. Palestine: Kairos Palestine, 2009.

Katanacho, Yohanna. *The Land of Christ: A Palestinian Cry*. Eugene, OR: Wipf & Stock, 2013.

―――. "The Theological Contribution of the Palestinian Kairos Document." In *Religious Stereotyping and Interreligious Relations*, edited by Jesper Svartvik and Jakob Wirén, 195–205. New York: Palgrave MacMillan, 2013.

Keenan, William. "Rediscovering the Theological in Sociology: Foundations and Possibilities." *Theory, Culture and Society* 20 (2003) 19–42.

Kepel, Gilles. *The Revenge of God: The Resurgence of Islam, Christianity and Judaism in the Modern World*. Cambridge: Polity, 1994.

Kessler, Michael Jon, ed. *Political Theology for a Plural Age*. New York: Oxford University Press, 2013.

Kim, Sebastian C. H. *Theology in the Public Sphere: Public Theology as a Catalyst for Open Debate*. London: SCM, 2011.

Kim, Sebastian C. H., and Jonathan A. Draper, eds. *Liberating Texts: Sacred Scriptures in Public Life*. London: SPCK, 2008.

Kirwan, Michael. *Political Theology: An Introduction*. Minneapolis: Fortress, 2009.

Kittredge, Cynthia Briggs, Ellen Bradshaw Aitken, and Jonathan A. Draper, eds. *The Bible in the Public Square: Reading the Signs of the Times*. Minneapolis: Fortress, 2008.

Koopman, Nico. "Churches and Public Policy Discourses in South Africa." *Journal of Theology for Southern Africa* (2010) 41–56.

―――. "Public Theology as Prophetic Theology: More Than Utopianism and Criticism?" *Journal of Theology for Southern Africa* (2009) 117–30.

―――. "Public Theology in (South) Africa: A Trinitarian Approach." *International Journal of Public Theology* 1 (2007) 188–209.

―――. "Some Contours for Public Theology in South Africa." *International Journal of Public Theology* 14 (2010) 123–38.

Le Bruyns, Clint. "The Rebirth of Kairos Theology? A Public Theological Perspective." 2012. http://www.academia.edu/1484082/The_Rebirth_of_Kairos_Theology_A_Public_Theological_Perspective.

Le Roux, Harold. "Kairos, Palestine." *Journal of Theology for Southern Africa* (2012) 48–66.

Leonardo, Gary S. D. *The Kairos Documents*. Durban, SA: Ujamaa Centre for Biblical and Theological Community Development and Research, 2010.

Lilla, Mark. *The Stillborn God: Religion, Politics, and the Modern West*. New York: Vintage, 2007.

Lodge, David M., and Christopher Hamlin. *Religion and the New Ecology: Environmental Responsibility in a World in Flux*. Notre Dame: University of Notre Dame Press, 2006.

Logan, Willis. *The Kairos Covenant: Standing with South African Christians*. New York: Meyer-Stone, 1988.

Losonczi, Péter, Mika Luoma-Aho, and Aakash Singh. *The Future of Political Theology: Religious and Theological Perspectives*. Farnham: Ashgate, 2011.

Lyotard, Jean-François. *The Postmodern Condition: A Report on Knowledge*. Translated by Geoff Benington and Brian Massumi. Manchester: Manchester University Press, 1984.

March, W. Eugene. *God's Land on Loan: Israel, Palestine and the World*. Louisville: Westminster John Knox, 2007.

Martin, David. *Reflections on Sociology and Theology*. Oxford: Clarendon, 1997.

Bibliography

Martin, David, John Orme Mills, and W. S. F. Pickering. *Sociology and Theology: Alliance and Conflict*. Leiden: Brill, 2004.

Marty, Martin. "Two Kinds of Two Kinds of Civil Religion." In *American Civil Religion*, edited by Russel E. Richey and Donald E. Jones, 139–57. New York: Harper & Row, 1974.

Mathewes, Charles T. *A Theology of Public Life*. Cambridge: Cambridge University Press, 2007.

McFague, Sallie. *Blessed Are the Consumers: Climate Change and the Practice of Restraint*. Minneapolis: Fortress, 2013.

McGovern, Arthur F. *Liberation Theology and Its Critics: Toward an Assessment*. Maryknoll, NY: Orbis, 1989.

McGrath, Alister. *Mere Theology*. London: SPCK, 2010.

McGrath, Alister E. *The Re-Enchantment of Nature: Science, Religion and the Human Sense of Wonder*. London: Hodder & Stoughton, 2003.

McGraw, Bryan T. *Faith in Politics: Religion and Liberal Democracy*. Cambridge: Cambridge University Press, 2010.

McGuire, Meredith B. *Religion: The Social Context*. Belmont, CA: Wadsworth Thomson Learning, 2002.

Meadows, Donella H., and Club of Rome. *The Limits to Growth: A Report for the Club of Rome's Project on the Predicament of Mankind*. London: Earth Island, 1972.

Metz, Johann Baptist. *Faith in History and Society: Toward a Practical Fundamental Theology*. Translated by David Smith. London: Burns & Oates, 1980.

———. *A Passion for God: The Mystical-Political Dimension of Christianity*. Translated by J. Matthew Ashley. New York: Paulist, 1998.

Micklethwait, John, and Adrian Wooldridge. *God Is Back: How the Global Rise of Faith Is Changing the World*. London: Allen Lane, 2009.

Milbank, John. *Theology and Social Theory: Beyond Secular Reason*. Malden, MA: Blackwell, 2006.

Miller, Randolph Crump. *Empirical Theology: A Handbook*. Birmingham, AL: Religious Education, 1992.

Mills, C. Wright. *The Sociological Imagination*. Oxford: Oxford University Press, 2000.

Moltmann, Jürgen. *The Coming of God: Christian Eschatology*. Translated by Margaret Kohl. London: SCM, 1996.

———. *Ethics of Hope*. Translated by Margaret Kohl. Minneapolis: Fortress, 2012.

———. *God for a Secular Society: The Public Relevance of Theology*. Translated by Margaret Kohl. London: SCM, 1999.

———. "Political Theology." *Theology Today* 28 (1971) 6–23.

———. *The Way of Jesus Christ: Christology in Messianic Dimensions*. Translated by Margaret Kohl. London: SCM, 1990.

Murdoch, Iris. "The Darkness of Practical Reason." In *Existentialists and Mystics: Writings on Philosophy and Literature*, edited by Peter Conradi, 193–202. London: Chatto, 1998.

Murray, John Courtney. *We Hold These Truths*. Lanham, MD: Sheed & Ward, 2005.

Niebuhr, H. Richard. *Christ and Culture*. New York: HarperOne, 2001.

Niebuhr, Reinhold. *Moral Man and Immoral Society: A Study in Ethics and Politics*. New York: Scribner, 1960.

Nolan, Albert. "Kairos Theology." In *Doing Theology in Context: South African Perspectives*, edited by John W. de Gruchy and Charles Villa-Vicencio, 212–18. Maryknoll, NY: Orbis, 1994.

Bibliography

Northcott, Michael. *A Moral Climate: The Ethics of Global Warming*. Maryknoll, NY: Orbis, 2007.

Nowers, Jeff, and Néstor Medina, eds. *Theology and the Crisis of Engagement: Essays on the Relationship between Theology and the Social Sciences*. Eugene, OR: Pickwick, 2013.

O'Donovan, Oliver. *The Desire of the Nations: Rediscovering the Roots of Political Theology*. Cambridge: Cambridge University Press, 1999.

Paeth, Scott R., E. Harold Breitenberg Jr. , and Hak Joon Lee, eds. *Shaping Public Theology: Selections from the Writings of Max L. Stackhouse*. Grand Rapids: Eerdmans, 2014.

Parker, Ian, ed. *Social Constructionism, Discourse and Realism*. London: Sage, 1998.

Pearson, Clive. "The Quest for a Glocal Public Theology." *International Journal of Public Theology* 1 (2007) 151–72.

Petersen, Robin M. "Theological Reflection on Public Policy. Soweto to the Millennium: Changing Paradigms of South African Prophetic Theology." *Journal of Theology for Southern Africa* (1996) 76–81.

———. "Time, Resistance and Reconstruction: Rethinking *Kairos* Theology." PhD diss., University of Chicago, 1995.

Petrella, Ivan. *Beyond Liberation Theology: A Polemic*. London: SCM, 2008.

———. *The Future of Liberation Theology: An Argument and Manifesto*. Aldershot: Ashgate, 2004.

Phillips, Elisabeth. *Political Theology: A Guide for the Perplexed*. London: T. & T. Clark, 2012.

Preston, Ronald H. *Church and Society in the Late Twentieth Century*. London: SCM, 1983.

———. *Religion and the Ambiguities of Capitalism*. London: SCM, 1991.

Raheb, Mitri. *I Am a Palestinian Christian*. Minneapolis: Fortress, 1995.

Rauschenbusch, Walter. *A Theology for the Social Gospel*. Louisville: Westminster John Knox, 1997.

Rawls, John. *Political Liberalism*. New York: Columbia University Press, 2005.

Rieger, Joerg. *Opting for the Margins: Postmodernity and Liberation in Christian Theology*. Oxford: Oxford University Press, 2003.

Robertson, Roland. *Globalization: Social Theory and Global Culture*. London: Sage, 1992.

Rorty, Richard. *Philosophy and Social Hope*. London: Penguin, 1999.

Rossing, Barbara. "God Laments with Us: Climate Change, Apocalypse and the Urgent *Kairos* Moment." *The Ecumenical Review* 62 (2010) 119–30.

Rowland, Christopher. *The Cambridge Companion to Liberation Theology*. Cambridge: Cambridge University Press, 2007.

Ruether, Rosemary Radford. *Sexism and God-Talk: Towards a Feminist Theology*. London: SCM, 1983.

Santmire, H. Paul. *The Travail of Nature: The Ambiguous Ecological Promise of Christian Theology*. Philadelphia: Fortress, 1985.

Schmid, Muriel. "From the Church of the Nativity to the Churches of the World: Palestinian Christians and Their "Cry of Hope."" *Theology Today* 69 (2013) 428–40.

Schmitt, Carl. *Political Theology: Four Chapters on the Concept of Sovereignty*. Cambridge, MA: MIT Press, 1985.

Scholte, Jan Aart. *Globalization: A Critical Introduction*. Basingstoke: Palgrave Macmillian, 2005.

Schreiter, Robert J. *The New Catholicity: Theology between the Global and the Local*. Maryknoll, NY: Orbis, 1997.

Bibliography

Scott, Peter, and William T. Cavanaugh. *The Blackwell Companion to Political Theology*. Malden, MA: Blackwell, 2004.
Segundo, Juan Luis. *Liberation of Theology*. Translated by John Drury. Maryknoll, NY: Orbis, 1976.
Seierstad, Åsne. *The Bookseller of Kabul*. Translated by Ingrid Christophersen. London: Virago, 2004.
Sennett, Richard. *The Fall of Public Man*. London: Faber and Faber, 1993.
Shahan, Michael, ed. *A Report from the Front Lines: Conversations on Public Theology*. Grand Rapids: Eerdmans, 2009.
Sipiora, Phillip, and James S. Baumlin, eds. *Rhetoric and Kairos: Essays in History, Theory, and Praxis*. Albany: State University of New York Press, 2002.
Smit, Dirkie, ed. *Essays in Public Theology*. Stellenbosch: Sun, 2007.
———. "Notions of the Public and Doing Theology." *International Journal of Public Theology* 1 (2007) 431–54.
Smith, Christian. *The Emergence of Liberation Theology: Radical Religion and Social Movement Theory*. Chicago: University of Chicago Press, 1991.
Stackhouse, Max L. *God and Globalization*. Vol. 4, *Globalization and Grace*. New York: Continuum, 2007.
———. "Public Theology and Ethical Judgement." In *Shaping Public Theology: Selections from the Writings of Max L. Stackhouse*, edited by Scott R. Paeth et al., 116–32. Grand Rapids: Eerdmans, 2014.
———. "Public Theology and Ethical Judgement." *Theology Today* 54 (2006) 165–91.
———. "Public Theology and Political Economy in a Globalizing Era." In *Public Theology for the 21st Century: Essays in Honour of Duncan B. Forrester*, edited by William F. Storrar and Andrew R. Morton, 179–94. London: T. & T. Clark, 2004.
Stark, Rodney. *The Rise of Christianity: A Sociologist Reconsiders History*. Princeton: Princeton University Press, 1996.
Storrar, William F. "The Naming of Parts: Doing Public Theology in a Global Era." *International Journal of Public Theology* 5 (2011) 23–43.
———. "Scottish Civil Society and Devolution: The New Case for Ronald Preston's Defense of Middle Axioms." In *The Future of Christian Social Ethics: Essays on the Work of Ronald H. Preston 1913–2001*, edited by Elaine Graham and Esther D. Reed, 37–46. London: Continuum, 2004.
Storrar, William F., and Andrew R. Morton, eds. *Public Theology for the 21st Century: Essays in Honour of Duncan B. Forrester*. London: T. & T. Clark, 2004.
Stout, Jeffrey. *Democracy and Tradition*. Princeton: Princeton University Press, 2004.
———. *Ethics after Babel: The Languages of Morals and Their Discontents*. Princeton: Princeton University Press, 2001.
Sweetman, Brendan. *Why Politics Needs Religion: The Place of Religious Arguments in the Public Square*. Downers Grove, IL: IVP Academic, 2006.
Tanner, R. E. S., and Colin Mitchell. *Religion and the Environment*. New York: Palgrave, 2002.
Taylor, Charles. *Modern Social Imaginaries*. Durham: Duke University Press, 2004.
———. "A Secular Age." Cambridge, MA: Belknap, 2007.
Temple, William. *Christianity and Social Order*. London: Shepard-Walwyn, 1976.
Thiemann, Ronald F. *Constructing a Public Theology*. Louisville: Westminster John Knox, 1991.

Bibliography

———. "The Public Theologian as Connected Critic: The Case of Central European Churches." In *A Report from the Front Lines: Conversations on Public Theology*, edited by Michael Shahan, 105–19. Grand Rapids: Eerdmans, 2009.
Tillich, Paul. *The Protestant Era*. Chicago: University of Chicago Press, 1957.
———. *Systematic Theology: Combined Volume*. Welwyn: Nisbet, 1968.
Tracy, David. *The Analogical Imagination: Christian Theology and the Culture of Pluralism*. New York: Crossroad, 1981.
———. *Blessed Rage for Order: The New Pluralism in Theology*. Chicago: University of Chicago Press, 1996.
———. "Defending the Public Character of Theology." *Christian Century* 98 (1981) 350–56.
True, David. "Embracing Hauerwas? A Niebuhrian Takes a Closer Look." *Political Theology* 8 (2007) 197–212.
United Nations. "Universal Declaration of Human Rights." In *The Philosophy of Human Rights*, edited by Patrick Hayden, 353–58. St. Paul: Paragon, 2001 [1948].
Vallier, Kevin. *Liberal Politics and Public Faith: Beyond Separation*. New York: Routledge, 2014.
Ven, Johannes A. van der. *Practical Theology: An Empirical Approach*. Kampen: Kok Pharos, 1993.
Ven, Johannes A. van der, and Michael Scherer-Rath. *Normativity and Empirical Research in Theology*. Boston: Brill, 2004.
Villa-Vicencio, Charles, ed. *Theology and Violence: The South African Debate*. Grand Rapids: Eerdmans, 1988.
Visser 't Hooft, W. A., and J. H. Oldham. *The Church and Its Function in Society*. Chicago: Willet & Clerk, 1937.
Volf, Miroslav. *A Public Faith: How Followers of Christ Should Serve the Common Good*. Grand Rapids: Brazos, 2011.
Volkmer, Ingrid. *The Global Public Sphere: Public Communication in the Age of Reflective Interdependence*. Cambridge: Polity, 2014.
Vries, Hent de, and Lawrence E. Sullivan, eds. *Political Theologies: Public Religions in a Post-Secular World*. New York: Fordham University Press, 2006.
Ward, Graham. *The Politics of Discipleship: Becoming Postmaterial Citizens*. London: SCM, 2009.
Warner, Michael. *Publics and Counterpublics*. New York: Zone, 2002.
Weber, Max. *The Sociology of Religion*. Translated by Ephraim Fischoff. London: Methuen, 1965.
Wells, Samuel, and Ben Quash. *Introducing Christian Ethics*. Chichester: Wiley-Blackwell, 2010.
West, Gerald. "Tracing the 'Kairos' Trajectory from South Africa (1985) to Palestine (2009): Discerning Continuities and Differences." *Journal of Theology for Southern Africa* 143 (July 2012) 4–22.
White, Lynn T. "The Historical Roots of Our Ecological Crisis." *Science* 155 (1967) 1203–7.
Williams, Rowan. *Faith in the Public Square*. London: Bloomsbury, 2012.
Wolterstorff, Nicholas. *The Mighty and the Almighty: An Essay in Political Theology*. Cambridge: Cambridge University Press, 2012.
Younan, Munib. *Witnessing for Peace: In Jerusalem and the World*. Minneapolis: Fortress, 2003.

www.ingramcontent.com/pod-product-compliance
Lightning Source LLC
Chambersburg PA
CBHW071458150426
43191CB00008B/1386